D0188648

WHAT IS
SARBANES-OXLEY?

WHAT IS SARBANES-OXLEY?

GUY P. LANDER

McGraw-Hill

New York Chicago San Francisco Lisbon London
Madrid Mexico City Milan New Delhi San Juan
Seoul Singapore Sydney Toronto

The **McGraw·Hill** Companies

Copyright © 2004 by Guy P. Lander. All rights reserved. Printed in the United States of America. Except as permitted under the United States Copyright Act of 1976, no part of this publication may be reproduced or distributed in any form or by any means, or stored in a database or retrieval system, without the prior written permission of the publisher.

5 6 7 8 9 0 FGR FGR 0 9 8 7 6 5

ISBN 0-07-143796-7

Editorial and production services provided by CWL Publishing Enterprises, Inc., Madison, Wisconsin, www.cwlpub.com.

This publication is designed to provide accurate and authoritative information in regard to the subject matter covered. It is sold with the understanding that neither the author nor the publisher is engaged in rendering legal, accounting, or other professional service. If legal advice or other expert assistance is required, the services of a competent professional person should be sought.
> —*From a Declaration of Principles jointly adopted by a Committee of the American Bar Association and a Committee of Publishers*

McGraw-Hill books are available at special quantity discounts to use as premiums and sales promotions, or for use in corporate training programs. For more information, please write to the Director of Special Sales, McGraw-Hill, Two Penn Plaza, New York, NY 10128. Or contact your local bookstore.

 This book is printed on recycled, acid-free paper containing a minimum of 50% recycled de-inked fiber.

FOR HAROLD AND RACHEL AND ROSANNE

CONTENTS

PREFACE

The many recent reforms in corporate governance were the result of large, well-publicized financial frauds. In response to those frauds, Congress passed the Sarbanes-Oxley Act of 2002, the Securities and Exchange Commission adopted many new rules and the major stock markets, including the New York Stock Exchange and Nasdaq Stock Market, changed their standards governing listed companies. This latticework of reforms has resulted in a new corporate governance regime, no longer market-driven and now highly rule-driven. This book presents this material in an organized way to enable the reader to understand the various requirements that apply in each area.

At the time of this writing, some rules and listing standards had not yet been formally adopted. Consequently, the proposals have been described in detail as the final rules and standards are not expected to vary much from the proposals.

ACKNOWLEDGMENTS

This book has benefited from the work of my colleagues at Davies Ward Phillips & Vineberg LLP who have helped me in various aspects of the material covered here as we struggled with the blizzard of regulatory initiatives. Thank you to Denis Frawley, Christian Lucky, Charles Malone, Gerald Shepherd, Scott Tayne, Jennifer Toone, and Corinne Weissberg.

Most of all, thank you to my children, Harold and Rachel, and wife, Rosanne, whose support, encouragement, and love make everything I do possible.

ABOUT THE AUTHOR

Guy P. Lander is a partner at Davies Ward Phillips & Vineberg LLP in New York City, where he specializes in corporate and securities law for international and domestic companies and financial institutions. Over the years, his practice has emphasized a wide range of financial transactions, including U.S. and international public and private offerings, listing foreign companies on U.S. exchanges, private placements, Rule 144A placements, Regulation S offerings and MJDS offerings, venture capital financings, tender and exchange offers, mergers, and acquisitions. Mr. Lander's practice includes representing U.S. and non-U.S. public companies in their SEC reporting and other corporate matters, as well as providing corporate governance and Sarbanes-Oxley advice. He also devotes a significant part of his time to regulatory matters for financial services firms. Mr. Lander advises securities brokerage firms, money managers, and hedge funds on their structuring, documentation, compliance, business activities, and significant transactions.

Mr. Lander is the author of the highly regarded treatise *U.S. Securities Law for International Financial Transactions and Capital Markets* (2 vols., West Group). He is also the author of *Resales of Restricted Securities Under SEC Rules 144 and 144A* (BNA Corporate Practice Series) and numerous articles for legal and securities industry journals.

Mr. Lander is the former Chairman of the Committee on Securities Regulation of the New York State Bar Association (NYSBA) and the former Chairman of NYSBA's Section on Business Law. He also participates in continuing legal education programs and is a frequent chair and speaker at programs sponsored by the NYSBA, including those on public offerings, private placements, and corporate governance.

AN OVERVIEW OF THE SARBANES-OXLEY ACT

On July 30, 2002, President George W. Bush signed the "Sarbanes-Oxley Act of 2002" (the "Act"), which amends the U.S. securities and other laws in significant ways. In 2001 and 2002 corporate giants like Enron, Global Crossing, and WorldCom were forced to declare bankruptcy, and massive accounting and other irregularities were revealed at those and other companies, such as Adelphi Communications. In response to the public outcry that ensued, the Act was enacted. The Act changed corporate governance, including the responsibilities of directors and officers, the regulation of accounting firms that audit public companies, corporate reporting, and enforcement. Many of the Act's provisions have been enhanced by SEC rulemaking and by stock market listing standards.

Generally, the Act applies to U.S. and non-U.S. public companies that have registered securities (debt or equity) with the SEC under the Securities Exchange Act of 1934 (the "Exchange Act").

WHAT THE ACT DOES

The Act establishes new law or changes existing law in many ways.

CORPORATE RESPONSIBILITY

Since the Act was enacted, there has been enhanced audit committee responsibility and auditor oversight, including prior approval for non-audit services by the auditor and the disclosure of all non-audit services of the auditor approved by the committee. CEOs and CFOs are now required to certify that their companies' annual and quarterly reports are accurate and not misleading, and that they have met their responsibility for evaluating internal controls. Additionally, there has been a ban on new personal loans by companies to their directors or executives (other than certain regular consumer loans).

AUDITOR INDEPENDENCE AND REGULATION OF AUDITORS

The Act has established new standards for determining auditor independence and created a new oversight board for the regulation of auditors. New audit standards include a prohibition against independent auditors providing many non-audit services (other than tax services) and mandatory audit partner rotation.

APPLICABILITY

Many of the Act's provisions apply to all companies (i.e., U.S. and non-U.S.) that are reporting companies (i.e., that have registered equity or debt securities with the SEC under the Exchange Act). However, some provisions apply only to companies that have equity securities listed on an exchange or on Nasdaq. Most provisions of the Act also apply to companies that have registered a public offering of their securities in the United States (and therefore are required to report under section 15(d) of the Exchange Act). In those cases, compliance may be required only during the period when they have the reporting obligation. Those companies that must file reports under the Exchange Act, either because they registered under the Exchange Act or because they registered a public offering of their securities in the United States, are referred to in this book as "reporting companies."

Given its complexity, the applicability of each section of the Act, and any SEC and exchange implementing rules must be carefully checked to determine if a specific provision applies to any particular situation.

ENHANCED DISCLOSURE

Generally both U.S. and non-U.S. companies are subject to the disclosure requirements of the Act, with some exceptions. The quality and timeliness of company information has been enhanced, including the following provisions:

1. Management and auditors must annually assess their company's internal controls and related disclosures.

2. Additional disclosure of off-balance sheet financing and financial contingencies is now required.

3. The presentation of pro forma information is now required.

4. Disclosure under Section 16 of the Exchange Act of insider stock transactions has been accelerated to two business days. (This does not apply to non-U.S. issuers.)

5. Disclosure of certain information will now be required in "real time."

OTHER PROVISIONS

Other provisions provide protections for the independence of security analysts and enhanced disclosure of their potential conflicts of interest. They also expanded SEC review of company reports, enhanced SEC enforcement powers, and increased penalties for securities law violations.

COMPLIANCE DATES

The Act provides for compliance dates for many of its provisions. Compliance dates have generally not been indicated for the provisions discussed in this book that are effective at the time of this writing.

MANAGEMENT CERTIFICATIONS

The Act contains two provisions that require senior management of a company to certify periodic reports filed with the SEC. Under Section 302 of the Act, the SEC adopted rules requiring the principal executive and financial officers of each reporting company to certify each periodic (i.e., quarterly and annual) report filed or submitted to the SEC (the "civil certifications"). Section 906 of the Act amended the U.S. Criminal Code to require each periodic report containing financial statements filed by a company under the Exchange Act to be accompanied by a certification of the chief executive officer and the chief financial officer of the company (the "criminal certification").

REPORTS COVERED

Under Section 302 of the Act and the related SEC rules, reporting companies must include Section 302 certifications by both the principal executive officer and the principal financial officer in each periodic (i.e., annual or quarterly) report filed or submitted to the SEC. The principal executive officer and principal financial officer must sign the certification themselves. The certification cannot be signed by another executive under a power of attorney.

CONTENT OF CERTIFICATION

Section 302 and related SEC Rules require the certification to cover the review of the report, its material accuracy, the fair presentation of financial information, disclosure controls, and internal accounting controls.

Paragraph 1 requires the certifying officer to state that he or she has reviewed the report being filed.

Paragraph 2 addresses the material accuracy and completeness of the information in the report. The officer must state that, based on his or her knowledge, the report does not contain any false statement or misleading omission of a material fact for the period covered by the report. This certification tracks Rule 10b-5, the general anti-fraud rule under the Exchange Act. The certification also tracks Rule 12b-20 under the Exchange Act, which requires Exchange Act reports to include whether additional information beyond that specifically required by the forms and rules is necessary to prevent the report from being misleading.

Paragraph 3 addresses the fair presentation of financial statements and other financial information. The officer must state that, based on his or her knowledge, the financial statements and other financial information included in the report fairly present in all material respects the financial condition, results of operations, and cash flows of the company for the periods presented in the report. This statement separately clarifies that the covered financial disclosure includes financial statements (and footnotes), selected financial data, management's discussion and analysis of financial condition and results of operations, and other financial information in a report. The statement that the overall financial disclosure "fairly presents" in all material respects the company's financial condition, results of operations, and cash flows is not limited to a representation that the financial statements and other financial information have been presented in accordance with GAAP (generally accepted accounting principles). Rather, this statement is intended to provide assurances that the financial information in a report, viewed in its entirety, is overall materially accurate and complete. Here, a "fair presentation" of a company's financial condition, results of operations, and cash flows is broader than financial reporting requirements under GAAP. The financial information will be viewed in its entirety in making this determination.

Paragraph 4 addresses "disclosure controls and procedures" and "internal control over financial reporting." The officer must state that he or she and the other certifying officers:

- ❏ Are responsible for establishing and maintaining "disclosure controls and procedures" and "internal control over financial reporting" for the company.

- ❏ Have designed the disclosure controls and procedures designed under their supervision), to ensure that material information about the company (including its consolidated subsidiaries) is made known to them by others within the entities, particularly during the period that the report covers.

- ❏ Have designed the internal control over financial reporting (or had the internal control over financial reporting designed under their supervision), to provide reasonable assurance that the financial statements conform to GAAP.

- ❏ Have evaluated the effectiveness of the company's disclosure controls and procedures and presented in the report their conclusions about the effectiveness of these controls and procedures.

❑ Have disclosed in the report any change in the company's internal controls over financial reporting that occurred during the period covered by the annual report that has materially affected, or is reasonably likely to materially affect, the company's internal controls over financial reporting

Paragraph 5 addresses disclosure concerning "internal control over financial reporting." The officers must state that they and the other certifying officers, based on their most recent evaluation of internal control over financial reporting, have disclosed to the company's auditors and the audit committee of the board of directors all significant deficiencies and material weaknesses in the design or operation of the internal control over financial reporting that are reasonably likely to adversely affect the company's ability to record, process, summarize, and report financial information. They must also disclose any fraud (even if not material) that involves management or other employees with a significant role in the company's internal control over financial reporting.

FORM OF CERTIFICATION

The disclosure rules described above require certifications for internal controls over financial accounting. First, "material weaknesses" must be disclosed to the audit committee and the independent auditor quarterly (annually for foreign private issuers) and to the public in the annual report on internal controls. Second, "significant deficiencies" must be disclosed to the audit committee and independent auditor quarterly (annually for foreign private issuers), but the rules do not require public disclosure of "significant deficiencies" if they are not also "material weaknesses." Third, any fraud, whether or not material, that involves internal control personnel must be disclosed to the audit committee and independent auditor quarterly (annually for foreign private issuers), but the rules do not specifically require public disclosure of such fraud. Last, "material changes" must be disclosed to the public quarterly (annually for foreign private issuers).

The rules prevent management from determining that a company's internal controls over financial reporting are satisfactory if it identifies one or more material weaknesses in the these controls over financial reporting. The terms "material weakness" and "significant deficiency" both represent deficiencies in the design or operation of internal controls that could adversely affect a company's ability to record, process, summarize, and report financial data consistent with the assertions of management. A "material weakness" constitutes a greater deficiency than a "significant deficiency." Because of this relationship, an aggregate of significant deficiencies could constitute a material weakness in a company's internal control over financial reporting.

The certification must be in the exact form set forth in the amendments to the affected reports. The wording of the required certification may not be changed, even if the change is inconsequential.

LIABILITY FOR FALSE SECTION 302 CERTIFICATION

Because the Section 302 certification is deemed to be "filed" under the Exchange Act, the Section 302 certification is subject to potential civil liability under Section 18 of the Exchange Act. It is also automatically incorporated into certain Securities Act filings, which creates Section 11 liability for registration statements filed under the Securities Act.

Additionally, an officer providing a false certification could be subject to SEC action for violating the reporting requirements of the Exchange Act and to both SEC and private actions for violating the fraud provisions of the securities laws of the Exchange Act. Additionally, a company's principal executive and financial officers, as signatories to the company's reports, may be liable for material misstatements or misleading omissions under general antifraud standards and under the SEC's authority to seek redress against those who cause, aid, or abet securities law violations.

SECTION 906 CERTIFICATION

Section 906 of the Act amended the Federal Criminal Code and imposed the so-called "criminal" certification for chief executive officers and chief financial officers of reporting companies (U.S. and non-U.S.) for certain periodic reports. The Section 906 certification must accompany periodic reports containing financial statements filed by a reporting company under the Exchange Act. This includes annual reports (i.e., Form 10-K, 10-Q, 20-F, and 40-F and any amendments to them) but not current reports (i.e., Form 6-K or 8-K), even if they contain financial statements.

The Section 906 certification requires the chief executive officer and the chief financial officer to certify that the report containing the financial statement fully complies with the reporting requirements of the Exchange Act. It also requires them to certify that information contained in the report fairly presents, in all material respects, the financial condition and results of operations of the company. Unlike the Section 302 Certification, the SEC has not mandated specific language for the Section 906 Certification.

Although it may take the form of a single statement signed by both officers, the CEO and the CFO are advised to complete separate certifications. A certification containing a knowledge qualification should satisfy the requirements of Section 906, although companies may wish to consider the public relations consequences of including such a qualification. However, the "fully complies" element of the certification must be made without a materiality qualification. The "fairly presents" element of the certification, while qualified by materiality, covers all information in the report, not just financial information. Like paragraph 3 of the Section 302 certification, it is not qualified by GAAP.

METHOD OF SUBMISSION

The Section 906 certification is furnished as an exhibit in all periodic reports containing financial statements. The requirement to furnish Section 906 certifications as exhibits enables the SEC, the Department of Justice, and the public to monitor the certifications and preserve possible evidence in the event of prosecution. The certification is automatically deemed "furnished," rather than "filed," with the SEC, thereby avoiding civil liability under Section 18 of the Exchange Act. Additionally, the Section 906 certification is not automatically incorporated by reference into a company's Securities Act registration statement, which also avoids liability under Section 11 of the Securities Act, unless the company explicitly incorporates the certification in a registration statement. A failure to furnish the Section 906 certifications would cause the periodic report to which they relate to be incomplete, thereby violating Section 13(a) of the Exchange Act.

AMENDMENTS

Unlike the Section 302 certifications, the Section 906 certifications are required only in periodic reports that contain financial statements. Consequently, amendments to periodic reports that do not contain financial statements would not require a new Section 906 certification but would require a new Section 302 certification to be filed with the amendment. Additionally, unlike the Section 302 certification, the Section 906 certification may take the form of a single statement signed by a company's chief executive and financial officers.

PENALTIES

Anyone who certifies any statement in the Section 906 certification knowing that the periodic report accompanying Section 906 does not comply with all the requirements of Section 906 (i.e., a "defective" certification) will be fined up to $1,000,000, imprisoned not more than 10 years, or both. Anyone who willfully certifies any statement in the Section 906 certification knowing that the accompanying report does not comply with all the requirements of the Section 906 will be fined not more than $5,000,000, imprisoned not more than 20 years, or both. Additionally, a violation of the Act is also a violation of the Exchange Act. Therefore, a failure to provide the required Section 906 certification, if done willfully, would be prosecuted as a criminal violation under Section 32 of the Exchange Act, which provides for fines of up to $5,000,000 and imprisonment up to 20 years.

CHAPTER 2

DISCLOSURE CONTROLS AND PROCEDURES

The Act and its related SEC rules require companies to maintain procedures to evaluate and make certain disclosures concerning their "disclosure controls and procedures" and "internal control over financial reporting." Reporting companies must also include an attestation from their auditors confirming management's conclusions in its evaluation of the internal control over financial reporting.[1]

DISCLOSURE CONTROLS AND PROCEDURES

DEFINITION

"Disclosure controls and procedures" are defined as a company's controls and other procedures designed to ensure that information required to be disclosed in its Exchange Act reports is recorded, processed, summarized, and reported within the required time periods. "Disclosure controls and procedures" include those controls and procedures that are designed to ensure that information a company is required to disclose in its Exchange Act reports is gathered and communicated to management (including its principal executive and financial officers) soon enough to allow timely decisions about required disclosure. They should also be designed to ensure that the reports are accurate, complete, and filed on time.

Disclosure controls and procedures must be designed, maintained, and evaluated to ensure that all information required to be submitted in a report is fair and accurate and that the report is filed in a timely manner. Consequently, the scope of the required disclosure controls and procedures is broader than the certification requirement. A company that fails to maintain the controls and procedures could be subject to SEC enforcement action even if the failure does not result in a flawed disclosure.

EVALUATION OF DISCLOSURE CONTROLS AND PROCEDURES

SEC rules also require that a company, under the supervision of the principal executive and financial officers, evaluate the effectiveness of the design and operation of the disclosure controls and procedures at the end of the period covered by any quarterly or annual report filed under the Exchange Act. The certifying officers must also present in the report their conclusions about the effectiveness of the disclosure controls and procedures based on their evaluation.

The SEC did not require any particular procedures for conducting the review and evaluation of the company's disclosure controls and procedures. Rather, each company is expected to develop a process that is consistent with its business, internal management, and supervisory practices. However, the SEC did recommend that a company create a disclosure committee responsible for considering the materiality of information and determining disclosure obligations on a timely basis. Such a committee should report to senior management, including the principal executive and financial officers, who bear express responsibility for designing, establishing, maintaining, reviewing, and evaluating the disclosure controls and procedures. While the evaluation is of effectiveness overall, a company's management may make judgments that evaluations, particularly quarterly evaluations, should focus on developments since the most recent evaluation, areas of weakness, or continuing concern or other aspects of disclosure controls and procedures that merit attention.[2]

DEVELOPING PROCEDURES

Companies' disclosure controls and procedures should be designed carefully. Senior management should be involved in supervising the design and operation of the procedures. The procedures should be written and provide guidance, and they should be tailored to the company's management structure, industry, and business processes. A central person or committee should oversee the procedures. And then senior management should formally review and evaluate these procedures for effectiveness. They must do this quarterly for U.S. companies and annually for non-U.S. companies.

The documentation for the procedures should include the following:

❏ The reports covered by the procedures.

❏ The people responsible for each section of the reports.

❏ The business units or departments involved.

❏ How these units or departments collect the information to be disclosed.

❏ How the information collected is communicated to those responsible for preparing the report.

❏ Materiality thresholds.

❏ How the process relates to the financial reporting system.

❏ How draft reports are reviewed and revised, including review by outside advisors, such as auditors, other experts, and outside counsel, and by the board of directors or audit committee.

❏ Checklist and timeline for the various steps.

In reviewing the disclosure controls and procedures, a company should consider:

❏ Whether the right people are involved and how carefully they review the reports.

❏ Whether the procedures allow enough time to prepare full and accurate disclosure.

❏ How the procedures ensure the accuracy of the reports.

❏ How key risk areas are identified and addressed.

❏ Where the system might fail and how to address those weaknesses.

❏ Whether any concerns have been raised by the SEC or others about the company's disclosure and how the company has addressed these issues.

The information gathered should be consistent with that published elsewhere by the company, such as in press releases and Web site postings.

The CEO and CFO (and others in top management) must be personally involved in the disclosure process. The CEO and CFO should review all reports requiring their certification, review specific issues addressed in the report, talk with key people who prepared the report, and review reports with appropriate third parties. The CEO and CFO should ask the main people preparing the reports whether they believe the disclosure is fair, accurate, and complete or if they think any part of the disclosure is questionable. Management may then review the results with the audit committee and independent auditors.

Companies should consider whether to create an employee "disclosure committee" responsible for considering the materiality of information and determining disclosure obligations on a timely basis. The SEC recommends that a company have such a committee. A member of the committee should be designated the coordinator of the disclosure procedures, responsible for its written documentation and its updates. The chair of the committee would coordinate the substance of the disclosure committee's considerations and ensure the appropriate involvement of the CEO and CFO. Companies should also consider whether someone on the disclosure committee should attend management or budget meetings.

Whether to obtain appropriate support, such as certifications from certain officers, to support those of the CEO and CFO is up to individual companies. Back-up certifications may be useful for some companies but not appropriate for others. The same is true for whether to engage third-party support, such as from their auditors or outside counsel, for their disclosure controls and procedures.

Companies should consider whether any areas of disclosure should have a small subcommittee to focus particularly on those disclosures.

MANAGEMENT EVALUATION OF THE CONTROLS

The CEO and the CFO must evaluate the effectiveness of the company's disclosure controls and procedures at the end of the period covered by each report, certify in the report that they did so, and present in the report their conclusions about the effectiveness of the procedures. The disclosure committee could conduct this evaluation. If companies have not chosen to have a disclosure committee, then those persons primarily responsible for disclosure matters might conduct the evaluation. In conducting this evaluation, the disclosure committee should do the following:

❏ Meet with the key people involved with disclosure in each business unit to discuss their unit's disclosure and ascertain whether they believe that the disclosure controls and procedures are effective in ensuring that information likely to be important is in fact disclosed to senior management.

❏ Meet with the board of directors or the audit committee, as appropriate, to review the design and operation of the procedures.

❏ Meet with independent auditors or outside counsel, as appropriate, to review the design and operation of the procedures.

❏ Prepare a written report evaluating the effectiveness of the design and operation of the procedures.

The CEO and CFO should each participate in these activities of the disclosure committee, whether or not they are members of this committee. Alternatively, they should at least review the evaluation reports and direct all necessary follow-up. After reviewing the report, the CEO and CFO should amend it as necessary for inclusion in the report being filed.

INTERNAL CONTROL OVER FINANCIAL REPORTING

All reporting companies are required to include in their annual reports a report of management on the company's internal control over financial reporting.[3] The auditor then must attest to, and report on, management's assessment of the effectiveness of the company's internal control over financial reporting. The auditor will also require the company to develop and maintain evidence to support management's assessment.

DEFINITION

"Internal control over financial reporting" means a process designed by, or under the supervision of, the company's principal executive and principal financial officers and implemented by the company's board of directors, management, and other personnel to provide reasonable assurance for the reliability of financial reporting and the preparation of financial statements for external purposes in accordance with generally accepted accounting principles. This includes those policies and procedures that:

1. Cover maintaining records, in reasonable detail, that accurately and fairly reflect the transactions and dispositions of the company's assets;

2. Provide reasonable assurance that transactions are recorded as necessary to prepare financial statements in accordance with generally accepted accounting principles, and that receipts and expenditures of the company are made only under the authorizations of management and directors of the registrant; and

3. Provide reasonable assurance for the prevention or timely detection of unauthorized acquisition, use, or disposition of the company's assets that could materially affect the financial statements.

The Foreign Corrupt Practices Act required reporting companies to keep books and records, in reasonable detail, that accurately reflect transactions. That Act also required companies to maintain a "system of internal accounting controls" sufficient to provide reasonable assurance that transactions are executed in accordance with management's authorization. The Act also requires that transactions are recorded to permit financial statements to be prepared under GAAP. To maintain accountability for assets, access to assets is permitted only under management's authorization, recorded assets are compared with existing assets at reasonable intervals, and appropriate action is taken for any difference.

As described above, the Foreign Corrupt Practices Act covers not only financial reporting and accounting but also the prevention of unauthorized transactions and the safeguarding of assets.

Auditing Standards (AU) section 319 requires auditors to obtain an understanding of internal controls sufficient to plan an audit.[4] AU section 319 covers financial reporting, operational efficiency and compliance with laws.[5] However, the SEC's definition of "internal controls over financial reporting" is limited to the parts of AU section 319 that pertain to financial reporting.

Under the SEC definition, internal control over financial reporting should be designed to provide reasonable assurance that the company's transactions are properly authorized, the company's assets are safeguarded against unauthorized or improper use, and the company's transactions are properly recorded and reported, all in order to permit the preparation of the company's financial statements in accordance with GAAP.

In 1992, an organization called the Committee of Sponsoring Organizations (COSO) of the Treadway Commission (National Commission on Fraudulent Financial Reporting) published a report providing guidance to management, boards of directors, and auditors about internal controls. This guidance included criteria against which control systems can be assessed, as well as information on preparing management reports on the effectiveness of internal controls.[6] This report provided guidance to management and boards of directors, rather than to auditors. The definition of internal control and related concepts used in the report are consistent with AU section 319.

This SEC definition is a blend of the internal controls required under AU 319 and the Foreign Corrupt Practices Act. The SEC stated that this definition encompasses the internal controls addressed in the COSO report that pertain to financial reporting objectives and that the definition is consistent with the description of internal accounting controls in the Foreign Corrupt Practices Act.

MANAGEMENT'S ANNUAL INTERNAL CONTROL REPORT

The SEC rules do not specify the precise content of the management report on internal control, because the reports should be tailored to the company's circumstances. However, the report must contain the following:

❏ A statement that management is responsible for establishing and maintaining adequate internal control over financial reporting.

❏ A statement identifying the framework management used to conduct the evaluation of the effectiveness of the company's internal control over financial reporting.

❏ Management's assessment of the effectiveness of the company's internal control over financial reporting as of the end of the company's most recent fiscal year, including a statement as to whether or not the company's internal control over financial reporting is effective. This assessment must disclose any "material weaknesses" in the company's internal control over financial reporting identified by management. Management may not conclude that the company's internal control over financial reporting is effective if there are one or more material weaknesses in the company's internal control over financial reporting.

❏ A statement that the company's independent auditor has attested to, and reported on, management's assessment of the company's internal control over financial reporting.

FRAMEWORK FOR MANAGEMENT EVALUATION

The SEC rules require companies to identify the evaluation framework used by management to assess the effectiveness of the company's internal control over financial reporting. The rules do not prescribe the use of a particular evaluation framework. However, management must base its evaluation on a suitable, recognized control framework established by a body or group that has followed due-process procedures. The framework must:

❏ Be free from bias.

❏ Permit reasonably consistent qualitative and quantitative measures of a company's internal control.

❏ Be sufficiently complete so that those relevant factors that would alter a conclusion about the effectiveness of a company's internal factors are not omitted.

❏ Be relevant to an evaluation of internal control.[7]

PROCEDURES FOR MANAGEMENT EVALUATION

The new rules do not specify the method or procedures management must follow in performing its evaluation and internal control assessment. However, management's evaluation must be supported by "evidential matter." Evidential matter includes documentation for both the design of the internal controls and the testing processes that provide reasonable support for the evaluation of whether the control is designed to prevent or detect material misstatements or omissions, the conclusion that the tests were appropriately planned and performed, and the conclusion that the results of the tests were appropriately considered.

The company's auditor, who must attest to and report on management's assessment of the effectiveness of the company's internal control over financial reporting, also will require that the company develop and maintain evidence to support management's assessment.

QUARTERLY EVALUATIONS

Quarterly evaluations of internal control over financial reporting need not be as extensive as the annual assessment. However, management, with the participation of the CEO and CFO, must evaluate any change in the company's internal control over financial reporting that occurred during a fiscal quarter that has materially affected, or is reasonably likely to materially affect, the company's internal control over financial reporting.

AUDITOR ATTESTATION AND REPORT ON MANAGEMENT'S ASSESSMENT

Under Section 404 of the Act, the SEC requires the company's auditor to attest to and report on management's assessment of the effectiveness of the company's internal control over financial reporting. The auditor's report will have to state the auditor's opinion as to whether management's assessment of the effectiveness of the company's internal control over financial reporting is fairly stated in all material respects or include an opinion to the effect that an overall opinion cannot be expressed. If an overall opinion cannot be expressed, the auditor must explain why.

The company must also file the attestation report of the auditor as part of its annual report. The evaluation must be based on procedures sufficient both to evaluate its design and to test its operating effectiveness. The rules do not establish standards for the attestation report. The Public Company Accounting Oversight Board (PCAOB) has been charged with adopting the standards for attestation engagements.

Management and the auditors must coordinate their processes for documenting and testing the internal controls over financial reporting. Although the SEC rules on auditor independence prohibit an auditor from providing certain non-audit services to a client, auditors may assist management in documenting internal controls. However, when the auditor is engaged to assist management in documenting internal controls, management must be actively involved in the process. While coordination between management and the auditor is necessary, management cannot delegate to the auditor its responsibility to assess its internal controls over financial reporting.

DIFFERENCES BETWEEN INTERNAL CONTROL OVER FINANCIAL REPORTING AND DISCLOSURE CONTROLS AND PROCEDURES

The definition of internal control over financial reporting overlaps in important respects with the definition of disclosure controls and procedures. Disclosure controls and procedures are controls and other procedures that are designed to ensure that information required to be disclosed by the company in its reports is recorded, processed, summarized, and reported within the required time periods. Disclosure controls and procedures will include those components of internal control over financial reporting that ensure that transactions are recorded as necessary to prepare financial statements. However, disclosure controls and procedures may be designed to exclude some components of internal control over financial reporting. For example, a company might conclude that some components of internal control over financial reporting of the accurate recording of transactions and disposition of assets or the safeguarding of assets are not part of the company's disclosure controls and procedures.

EFFECTIVE DATES

Because of the substantial effort involved in complying with the new rules, the SEC adopted an extended transition period for compliance with the new annual report and disclosure requirements for internal control over financial reporting, based on the nature of the company.

A company that is an "accelerated filer" as of the end of the first fiscal year ending on or after June 15, 2004 must begin to comply with the new disclosure requirements in its annual report for that fiscal year (which, for calendar year companies, means the annual report for calendar year 2004 that will be due in early 2005).

Non-accelerated filers, including smaller companies and foreign private issuers, must begin to comply with the new disclosure requirements in their annual reports for their first fiscal year ending on or after April 15, 2005 (which, for calendar year companies, means the annual report for calendar year 2005 that will be due in early 2006).

A company must begin to comply with the quarterly evaluation requirements for changes to internal control over financial reporting for its first periodic report due after the first annual report that must include management's internal control report.

RECOMMENDATIONS

The extended delay before compliance is required gives companies time to satisfy the new requirements. Among the steps companies can take are the following:

❏ Consult with the auditor.

❏ Be sensitive to auditor independence concerns.

❏ Consider upgrading the internal audit function.

❏ Adopt a framework for conducting the required evaluation.

❏ Develop a form of disclosure report for the annual internal control report.

❏ Make sure the audit committee is brought into the process.

NOTES

1. The requirements for these procedures and their evaluation and certification are contained in Sections 302 and 404 of the Act, Rules 13a-15 and 15d-15 under the Exchange Act, and Items 307 and 308 of Regulations S-K and S-B. The terms "disclosure controls and procedures" and "internal control over financial reporting" are defined in Rules 13a-15 and 15d-15 under the Exchange Act.

2. Because foreign private issuers are not subject to quarterly reporting requirements under the Exchange Act, they are required to evaluate and disclose conclusions about the effectiveness of their disclosure controls and procedures only in their annual report (i.e., not quarterly).

3. Item 308 of Regulations S-K and S-B. These rules apply to foreign private issuers but not to registered investment companies or issuers of asset-backed securities.

4. AU section 319 defines "internal control" as follows: .06 Internal Control is a process—effected by an entity's board of directors, management, and other personnel—designed to provide reasonable assurance regarding the achievement of objectives in the following categories:

(a) reliability of financial reporting,

(b) effectiveness and efficiency of operations, and

(c) compliance with applicable laws and regulations.

5. See AICPA Codification of Statements on Auditing Standards ("AU") §319, at paragraph .06. Paragraph .07 contains the definition: .07 Internal control consists of five interrelated components:

(a) Control environment sets the tone of an organization, influencing the control consciousness of its people. It is the foundation for all other components of internal control, providing discipline and structure.

(b) Risk assessment is the entity's identification and analysis of relevant risks to achievement of its objectives, forming a basis for determining how the risks should be managed.

(c) Control activities are the policies and procedures that help ensure that management directives are carried out.

(d) Information and communication systems support the identification, capture, and exchange of information in a form and time frame that enable people to carry out their responsibilities.

(e) Monitoring is a process that assesses the quality of internal controls performance over time.

6. See "Internal Control—Integrated Framework" (July 1994, containing material originally published in September 1992 and supplemented in May 1994). The Commission consisted of representatives of the American Institute of Certified Public Accountants, the American Accounting Association, the Institute of Internal Auditors, the Institute of Management Accountants, and the Financial Executives Institute (now Financial Executives International). The Commission listed five interrelated components based on the COSO report.

1. Control Environment: Tone at the top—audit committee, management philosophy and style.

2. Risk Assessment: Identifying and dealing with business risks.

3. Control Activities: Detailed policies and procedures for ensuring that management's directives are carried out. Include general and application controls.

4. Information and Communication: Support the exchange of information to enable people to function.

5. Monitoring: Assess quality of performance.

7. These criteria are met by the evaluation framework contained in the 1992 COSO report. There are currently other evaluation standards outside the United States and evaluation frameworks other than COSO that may be developed within the United States that may meet the SEC's criteria for a suitable evaluation framework.

MANAGEMENT'S DISCUSSION AND ANALYSIS

Under Section 401(a) of the Act, the SEC adopted rules requiring disclosure of off-balance sheet arrangements in the Management's Discussion and Analysis of Financial Condition and Results of Operations (MD&A) section of SEC disclosure documents. The rules codify views previously expressed by the SEC on required disclosure of off-balance sheet arrangements. The rules require reporting companies (U.S. and non-U.S.) to explain their off-balance sheet arrangements in a separately captioned subsection of the MD&A section of their SEC disclosure documents containing financial statements.

Reporting companies must also include in the MD&A section a table summarizing certain contractual obligations, as well as provide additional disclosure for critical accounting policies and critical accounting estimates.

OFF-BALANCE SHEET DISCLOSURES

OFF-BALANCE SHEET ARRANGEMENTS DEFINED

Under SEC rules, an "off-balance sheet transaction" includes any transaction or contract with an unconsolidated entity, under which the company has:

1. Any obligation under certain guarantee contracts (i.e., guaran-

tees described in paragraph 3 of FASB Interpretation No. 45, Guarantor's Accounting and Disclosure Requirements for Guarantees, including Indirect Guarantees of Indebtedness of Others).

2. A retained or contingent interest in assets transferred to an unconsolidated entity or similar arrangement that serves as credit, liquidity, or market risk support to that other entity for such assets (e.g., a subordinated retained interest in a pool of receivables transferred to an unconsolidated entity that can provide credit support to the entity by cushioning the senior interests if part of the receivables becomes uncollectible).

3. Any obligation (including a contingent obligation) under certain derivative instruments (e.g., derivative instruments held or issued by a company that are indexed to the company's stock and classified as stockholders' equity under GAAP).

4. Any obligation (including a contingent obligation) under a material variable interest (as described in FASB Interpretation No. 46, Consolidation of Variable Interest Entities) held by the company in an unconsolidated entity that provides financing, liquidity, market risk, or credit risk support to the company, or engages in leasing, hedging, or research and development services with the company.[1]

This definition of "off-balance sheet arrangement" is intended to target the means through which companies typically structure off-balance sheet transactions or otherwise incur risks of loss that are not fully transparent to investors.

The rules apply only to contractual arrangements. Consequently, the disclosure obligations arise only when an unconditionally binding definitive agreement (subject to customary closing conditions) exists or, if there is no such agreement, when settlement of the transaction occurs. Generally, preliminary negotiations need not be disclosed in the MD&A. Contingent liabilities arising out of litigation, arbitration, or regulatory actions are not considered to be off-balance sheet arrangements.

DISCLOSURE THRESHOLD

The rules require disclosure of off-balance sheet arrangements that either have, or are "reasonably likely" to have, a current or future material effect on the company's financial condition, changes in financial condition, revenues or expenses, results of operations, liquidity, capital expenditures, or capital resources. Under this standard, disclosure of off-balance sheet arrangements can be avoided only if there is no reasonable likelihood of either the event occurring or its effect being material.

MANAGEMENT'S DETERMINATION OF WHETHER DISCLOSURE IS REQUIRED

To determine whether to disclose off-balance sheet arrangements, management must undertake the following analysis.

First, management must identify and critically analyze all the company's off-balance sheet arrangements, including its guarantee contracts, retained or contingent interests, derivative instruments, and variable interests.

Second, management must assess the likelihood of the occurrence of any known trend, demand, commitment, event, or uncertainty that could affect an off-balance sheet arrangement (e.g., performance of a guarantee, an obligation under a variable interest or equity-linked or indexed derivative instrument, or recognition of an impairment).

Third, if management concludes that the known trend, demand, commitment, event, or uncertainty that could affect an off-balance arrangement is not reasonably likely to occur, then the company need not disclose the off-balance sheet arrangement. (The company may still have to disclose the arrangement in the footnotes to the financial statements under other principles.)

Alternatively, if management cannot determine that the known trend, demand, commitment, event, or uncertainty is not reasonably likely to occur, it must evaluate objectively the consequences of the known item on the assumption that it will occur. Under this assumption that the known trend, demand, commitment, event, or uncertainty will occur, disclosure is required unless management concludes that the known item is not "reasonably likely" to have a material effect on the company's financial condition, changes in financial condition, revenues or expenses, results of operations, liquidity, capital expenditures, or capital resources.

The assessment must be objectively reasonable when the determination is made.

REQUIRED DISCLOSURE

Under the rules, companies must disclose the following information to the extent necessary for understanding a company's off-balance sheet arrangements and their effects:

- The nature and business purpose of the company's off-balance sheet arrangements.

- The importance of the off-balance sheet arrangements to the company for liquidity, capital resources, market risk or credit risk support or other benefits, the financial impact of the arrangements on the company and the risks associated with the arrangements, and any known event, demand, commitment, trend, or uncertainty that will or is reasonably likely to result in a termination or material reduction in availability of any off-balance sheet arrangements that provide material benefits to the company and the course of action that the company has taken or proposes to take.

Additionally, the company must provide other information that it believes to be necessary for an understanding of its off-balance sheet arrangements and their material effects on its financial condition, changes in financial condition, revenues or expenses, results of operations, liquidity, capital expenditures, or capital resources. The disclosure should provide investors with management's insight into the effect and proximity of the potential material risks that are reasonably likely to arise from material off-balance sheet arrangements.

Generally, the disclosure is required to address only the most recent fiscal year, but it should also discuss changes from the previous year, where necessary, for an understanding of the disclosure. Companies must aggregate off-balance sheet arrangements in groups or categories that increase understanding and discuss important distinctions in terms and effects of the aggregated arrangements.

The disclosure in the MD&A need not repeat information contained in the footnotes to the financial statements if the MD&A contains appropriate cross-references to the footnotes and integrates footnote disclosure into the discussion in a way that informs readers of the significance of the information not in the MD&A.

AGGREGATE CONTRACTUAL COMMITMENTS

TABULAR DISCLOSURE OF CONTRACTUAL OBLIGATIONS

All reporting companies (except for small business issuers) must disclose in a table in their annual reports their aggregate amounts of specified categories of contractual obligations broken out over time. The rules are intended to enable investors to assess a company's short-term and long-term liquidity and capital resources needs. The table, which is set forth below, must include information, as of the latest fiscal year end balance sheet date, aggregated by type of contractual obligation, for at least the periods specified in the table on the next page.

Companies may break down the specified categories into other categories suitable to their particular business, so long as their revised table includes all of the obligations that fall within the specified categories. Footnotes should be added to the table to the extent necessary for an understanding of the timing and amount of contractual obligations.

Except for "purchase obligations," the categories of contractual obligations are defined by the relevant U.S. GAAP accounting pronouncements that require disclosure of these obligations in the financial statements or footnotes.[2]

A "purchase obligation" means an agreement to purchase goods or services that is legally binding on the company and that specifies all significant terms. If the purchase obligations are subject to variable price provisions, then the company must provide estimates of the payments due. Therefore, the table should discuss any variable price provisions and any material termination or renewal provisions to the extent necessary to understand the timing and amount of the company's payment obligations.

Contractual Obligations	Total	Less than 1 Year	1-3 Years	3-5 Years	More than 5 Years
Long-Term Debt					
Capital (Finance) Lease Obligations					
Operating Leases					
Purchasing Obligations					
Other Long-Term Obligations Reflected on the Company's Balance Sheet under the GAAP of the Primary Financial Statements					
Total					

U.S. companies need not include the table in quarterly reports, but they would have to describe material changes outside the ordinary course of business in the specified categories of contractual obligations during the interim period.[3]

SAFE HARBOR FOR FORWARD LOOKING INFORMATION

The rules extend the statutory safe harbors for "forward-looking information" to the MD&A disclosure of the off-balance sheet arrangements and the table of contractual obligations required under the rules.

CRITICAL ACCOUNTING POLICIES: PROPOSED DISCLOSURE REQUIREMENTS

The SEC proposed additional disclosure requirements for a company's critical accounting policies. The proposals would require disclosure in two areas:

1. Accounting estimates made by a company applying its accounting policies, including quantification of sensitivity to different assumptions.

2. The initial adoption by a company of an accounting policy that has a material effect on the company's financial presentation.[4]

Under the first of the proposals, a company would have to identify in its MD&A and in its annual report those accounting estimates reflected in its financial statements that both required it to make assumptions about matters that were "highly uncertain" at the time of estimation and were sufficiently important. A matter is highly uncertain if it is dependent on events that are remote in time and that may or may not occur or it is not capable of being readily calculated from generally accepted methodologies or derived with some degree of precision from available data. A matter that is highly uncertain requires management to use significant judgment in making assumptions about the matter. An estimate is considered sufficiently important if either (a) different estimates that the company reasonably could have used in the current period or (b) changes in the accounting estimates that are reasonably likely to occur from period to period would have a material effect on the company's financial presentation (i.e., financial condition, changes in financial condition, or results of operations). The proposal would also require that the effect of changes in these critical accounting estimates be quantified. U.S. companies would also be required to update information in their quarterly reports.

The current proposals reflect the SEC's concern that, while financial statements convey the appearance of precision, they typically involve undisclosed judgments, estimates, and choices among alternative principles that make reported results potentially "fuzzier" than suggested by earnings-per-share figures calculated to two decimal places.

Some portions of existing accounting literature address disclosure about these types of matters under GAAP, but the SEC appears to believe more disclosure is required.

Section 204 of the Act requires that registered public accounting firms make timely reports to the audit committee of, among other things, "all critical accounting policies and practices to be used."

The proposed rules would require a separately captioned subsection in MD&A for annual financial statements, entitled "Application of Critical Accounting Policies." New MD&A disclosure would be required in annual reports and registration statements of U.S. and non-U.S. companies that contain an MD&A section. It would also be required in annual shareholder reports and proxy and information statements of U.S. companies. U.S. companies would also be required to update critical accounting disclosures for material changes in their quarterly reports.

The proposed rules would require disclosure about critical estimates made in applying accounting policies, including the quantification of sensitivity or disclosure of the range of reasonably possible estimates the company considered.

PROPOSED DISCLOSURE REQUIREMENTS

For each accounting estimate identified as critical, the company would be required to include the following information in the MD&A:

- ❏ **Description.** A discussion identifying and describing the estimate, the methodology used, certain assumptions, and reasonably likely changes.

- ❏ **Significance.** An explanation of the significance of the accounting estimate to the company's financial condition, changes in financial condition, and results of operations and, where material, an identification of the line items in the financial statements affected by the accounting estimate.

- ❏ **Quantification of Sensitivity.** A quantitative discussion of changes in line items in the financial statements and overall financial performance if the company were to assume that the accounting estimate was changed.

- ❏ **Historical Changes.** A quantitative and qualitative discussion of any material changes made to the accounting estimate in the past three years, the reasons for the changes, and the effect on line items in the financial statements and overall financial performance.

❏ **Audit Committee Discussion.** A statement of whether or not the company's senior management has discussed with the audit committee the development and selection of the accounting estimate and the relevant MD&A disclosure and, if no such audit committee discussion has occurred, the reasons for this.

❏ **Affected Segments.** If the company operates in more than one operating segment, an identification of the segments of the company's business the accounting estimate affects.

❏ **Segment-Specific Effects.** A discussion of the estimate on a segment basis, mirroring the one required on a company-wide basis, to the extent that a failure to present that information would result in an omission that renders the disclosure materially misleading.

INITIAL ADOPTION OF ACCOUNTING POLICIES

A company initially adopts an accounting policy when events or transactions that affect the company occur for the first time, when events or transactions that were previously immaterial in their effect become material, or when events or transactions occur that are clearly different from previous events or transactions. If an initially adopted accounting policy has a material effect on the company's financial condition or results of operations, that effect will likely be of interest to investors, to financial analysts, and to others.

The SEC proposed that at any time a company initially adopts an accounting policy having a material effect on its financial presentation, the company would have to disclose the events that gave rise to the adoption. This includes the accounting principle that has been adopted and the method of applying that principle, as well as the qualitative (but not quantitative) effect of the adoption and the choices the company had among accounting principles.

Last, if no accounting literature exists governing the accounting for the events or transactions giving rise to the initial adoption of a material accounting policy (e.g., unusual or unique events or transactions), the company would be required to explain its decision for the choice of accounting principle to use and which method to use for applying that principle.

DISCLOSING CHANGES TO EXISTING POLICIES

Under GAAP and current SEC rules, a company is already required to disclose when it changes an existing accounting policy. The company must determine that the alternative principle is preferable under the circumstances and must file a letter from its independent public accountant to that effect. It must also make certain to disclose in its financial statements about the accounting change the reasons for the change, including explaining why the newly adopted accounting principle is preferable.

Off-balance sheet arrangements covered by the definition must be discussed in the MD&A even if a company presents its primary financial statements under "home country" (i.e., non-U.S.) generally accepted accounting principles. Nevertheless, the definition of "off-balance sheet arrangements" in the new rules relies on certain concepts from U.S. GAAP. Therefore, to identify the types of arrangements that are subject to disclosure under the new rules, a foreign private issuer must assess its guarantee contracts and variable interests under U.S. GAAP. Foreign private issuers must already make this assessment when they reconcile or prepare their financial statements in accordance with U.S. GAAP. However, a foreign private issuer's MD&A disclosure should continue to focus on its primary financial statements, despite the fact that its various "off-balance sheet arrangements" have been defined by reference to U.S. GAAP.

A foreign private issuer that prepares financial statements under its home country GAAP should include contractual obligations in the table that are consistent with the classifications used in its home country GAAP (i.e., the GAAP under which its primary financial statements are prepared).

For a non-U.S. company, the table would only have to be in the annual report. The requirements would not apply to reports furnished by foreign private issuers on Form 6-K. Therefore, unless a foreign private issuer files a registration statement under the Securities Act of 1933 that must include interim financials statements and related MD&A disclosure, it need only update the MD&A disclosure annually.

In annual reports on Form 20-F and registration statements, the SEC proposes to apply to non-U.S. companies the same MD&A disclosure requirements for critical accounting estimates that would apply to U.S. companies. However, for those non-U.S. companies whose primary financial statements are non-U.S. GAAP, the proposed disclosure would follow the approach that now applies to MD&A disclosure by non-U.S. companies: the company would have to consider critical accounting estimates for both its primary financial statements and its reconciliation of those statements to U.S. GAAP. The proposed rules take a similar approach to disclosures by non-U.S. companies about the initial adoption of accounting policies.

NOTES

1. Off-balance sheet arrangements covered by the definition must be discussed in the MD&A even if a company presents its primary financial statements under "home country" (i.e., non-U.S.) generally accepted accounting principles. Nevertheless, the definition of "off-balance sheet arrangements" in the new rules relies on certain concepts from U.S. GAAP. Therefore, to identify the types of arrangements that are subject to disclosure under the new rules, a foreign private issuer must assess its guarantee contracts and variable interests under U.S. GAAP. Foreign private issuers must already make this assessment when they reconcile or prepare their financial statements in accordance with U.S. GAAP. However, a foreign private issuer's MD&A disclosure should continue to focus on its primary financial statements, despite the fact that its various "off-balance sheet arrangements" have been defined by reference to U.S. GAAP.

2. A foreign private issuer that prepares financial statements under its home country GAAP should include contractual obligations in the table that are consistent with the classifications used in its home country GAAP (i.e., the GAAP under which its primary financial statements are prepared).

3. For a non-U.S. company, the table would only have to be in the annual report. The requirements would not apply to reports furnished by foreign private issuers on Form 6-K. Therefore, unless a foreign private issuer files a registration statement under the Securities Act of 1933 that must include interim financials statements and related MD&A disclosure, it need only update the MD&A disclosure annually.

4. In annual reports on Form 20-F and registration statements, the SEC proposes to apply to non-U.S. companies the same MD&A disclosure requirements for critical accounting estimates that would apply to U.S. companies. However, for those non-U.S. companies whose primary financial statements are non-U.S. GAAP, the proposed disclosure would follow the approach that now applies to MD&A disclosure by non-U.S. companies: the company would have to consider critical accounting estimates for both its primary financial statements and its reconciliation of

those statements to U.S. GAAP. The proposed rules take a similar approach to disclosures by non-U.S. companies about the initial adoption of accounting policies.

NON-GAAP FINANCIAL MEASURES (REGULATION G)

In response to concerns over pro forma results that may mislead using non-GAAP financial measures, the SEC adopted rules to implement Sections 401(b) and 409 of the Act. A new disclosure regulation, Regulation G, was established; it requires public companies that disclose a non-GAAP financial measure (i.e., pro forma results) to include the most directly comparable GAAP financial measure and a reconciliation of the non-GAAP financial measure to the most directly comparable GAAP financial measure. Additionally, similar disclosure requirements for the use of non-GAAP financial measures in SEC filings was established. Last, an amendment on Form 8-K requires U.S companies to file with the SEC their earnings releases, i.e., disclosures of material non-public financial information about completed fiscal or quarterly periods.

REGULATION G

Regulation G applies to any company reporting under the Exchange Act whenever the company or anyone acting for it discloses any material information that includes a non-GAAP financial measure.[1] First, Regulation G provides that a non-GAAP financial measure, taken together with the accompanying information, may not be false or misleading. Second, Regulation G requires the company to provide a reconciliation by including the most directly comparable GAAP financial measure (e.g., earnings or cash flows as reported in GAAP financial statements) with the non-GAAP financial measure. Also, it must include a reconciliation (by schedule or other clearly understandable method) of the differences between the non-GAAP financial measure and the most directly comparable GAAP financial measure. The reconciliation must be quantitative for historic measures and for prospective measures quantitative to the extent available without unreasonable efforts.

For non-GAAP financial measures that are forward-looking, the required quantitative reconciliation must detail the differences between the forward-looking non-GAAP financial measure and the appropriate forward-looking GAAP financial measure on a schedule or other presentation. If there is no accessible forward-looking GAAP financial measure, the company must disclose that fact and provide any reconciling information that is available without an unreasonable effort. Further, the company must identify any information that is unavailable and disclose its probable significance.

If a non-GAAP financial measure is released orally, telephonically, in a webcast, in a broadcast, or by similar means, a company may provide the required accompanying information by posting it on the company's Web site and disclosing the location and availability of the required accompanying information during the presentation.

Regulation G will not apply to a non-GAAP financial measure included in disclosure for a proposed business combination, an entity resulting from a business combination, or an entity that is a party thereto if the disclosure is subject to the rules for business combination transactions.

DEFINITION OF NON-GAAP FINANCIAL MEASURE

Under Regulation G, a "non-GAAP financial measure" is a numerical measure of a company's historical or future financial performance, financial position, or cash flows that differs from the most directly comparable GAAP financial measure in the statement of income, balance sheet, or statement of cash flows.

"GAAP" refers to generally accepted accounting principles in the United States.[2]

Non-GAAP financial measures do not include financial measures required to be disclosed by GAAP, SEC rules, or other applicable regulatory systems. Non-GAAP financial measures also do not include operating and other statistical measures (e.g., unit sales or numbers of employees) and ratios or statistical measures calculated using only GAAP financial measures and operating measures. Non-GAAP financial measures also do not include financial information that does not have the effect of providing numerical measures different from comparable GAAP measures (e.g., amounts of expected indebtedness or estimated revenues or expenses of a new product line).

The definition of non-GAAP financial measure is intended to capture all measures that have the effect of depicting either a measure of performance different from that in the financial statements (e.g., income or loss before taxes) or a measure of liquidity different from cash flow or cash flow from operations computed under GAAP.

An example of a non-GAAP financial measure would be a measure of operating income that excludes one or more expense or revenue items as "non-recurring."

REGULATION G: LIABILITY

Regulation G is a disclosure requirement for all reporting companies (including non-U.S. companies, except for registered investment companies). Nothing in Regulation G affects any person's liability under the fraud provisions of the Exchange Act, i.e., Section 10(b) and Rule 10b-5. The facts and circumstances surrounding a material violation of Regulation G could give rise to a Section 10(b) or Rule 10b-5 violation if all the elements for such a violation were present.

USING NON-GAAP FINANCIAL MEASURES IN SEC FILINGS

Regulation S-K and Regulation S-B were amended to incorporate the requirements of Regulation G into SEC filings.[3] The Regulation S-K and Regulation S-B amendments require companies using a non-GAAP financial measure in SEC filings to provide:

❏ The most directly comparable GAAP financial measure presented with equal or greater prominence.

❑ A quantitative reconciliation (by schedule or other clearly understandable method) of the differences between the non-GAAP financial measure disclosed with the most directly comparable GAAP measure. (If the GAAP financial measure is not accessible on a forward-looking basis, the company must disclose that fact and provide reconciling information that is available without unreasonable effort.)

❑ A statement of the reasons why the company's management believes the non-GAAP financial measure provides useful information to investors.

❑ To the extent material, a statement of the additional purposes, if any, that are not otherwise disclosed for which the company's management uses the non-GAAP financial measure.

Additionally, the amendments to Regulation S-K (and Regulation S-B) prohibit any of the following:

1. Excluding charges or liabilities that required or will require cash settlement or would have required cash settlement absent an ability to settle in another manner, from non-GAAP liquidity measures, other than the measures EBIT and EBITDA. (However, companies must reconcile these measures to their most directly comparable GAAP measure.)

2. Adjusting a non-GAAP performance measure to eliminate or smooth items identified as non-recurring, infrequent, or unusual, when either the nature of the charge or gain is such that it is reasonably likely to recur or there was a similar change or gain within the prior two years.

3. Presenting non-GAAP financial measures on the face of the company's GAAP financial statements or in the accompanying notes.

4. Presenting non-GAAP financial measures on the face of any pro forma financial information required by Article 11 of Regulation S-X.

5. Using titles or descriptions of non-GAAP financial measures that are the same as, or confusingly similar to, titles or descriptions used for GAAP financial measures.

The rules do permit disclosure of non-GAAP per share financial measures. The rules also permit non-GAAP financial measures that are included in disclosures for a business combination, the disclosures by the entity resulting from the combination or by an entity that is a party to the combination, if the disclosures are in a communication subject to the communication rules for business combinations.

The term "non-GAAP financial measure" is the same here as it is for Regulation G.[4]

FORM 8-K: FILING EARNINGS RELEASE

The addition of a new Item 12 to Form 8-K brings earnings releases into the formal disclosure system. Form 8-K now requires companies to file earnings releases with the SEC within five business days of any public disclosure of material non-public information about the company's results of operations or financial condition for a completed annual or quarterly fiscal period, regardless of whether the earnings release contains non-GAAP financial measures. The company would briefly identify the announcement or release on the Form 8-K and file a copy as an exhibit. The new filing requirement is triggered by a company's earnings announcement and release for a completed fiscal year or quarter that was not previously disclosed. The new rule does not require that companies issue earnings releases.[5]

If non-public information is disclosed orally, telephonically, or by webcast, broadcast, or similar means, form 8-K provides an exception from filing under all of the following conditions:

1. The disclosure initially occurs within 48 hours of a written release or announcement furnished to the SEC on Form 8-K under Item 12.

2. The presentation is broadly accessible to the public by dial-in conference call, webcast, or similar technology.

3. The financial and statistical information contained in the presentation is provided on the company's Web site, with any information that would be required under Regulation G.

4. The presentation was announced by a widely disseminated press release that included instructions as to when and how to access

the presentation and the location on the company's Web site where the information would be available.

The rule does not apply to disclosure of earnings estimates for future periods, unless those estimates are in the public announcement of material non-public information concerning an annual or quarterly period that has ended.

Earning announcements and releases are also subject to Regulation FD. Similar to disclosure under Regulation FD, historical information submitted under Item 12 of Form 8-K would be considered "furnished" with the SEC for liability purposes rather than "filed." Additionally, a Form 8-K filed under Item 12 would meet a company's obligation under Regulation FD only if it were filed within the time requirements of Regulation FD.

NOTES

1. Regulation G applies to foreign private issuers, with one limited exception. Regulation G does not apply to public disclosure of a non-GAAP financial measure by a foreign private issuer if the following three conditions are met:

   (a) the issuer's securities are listed or quoted on a securities market (i.e., an exchange or inter-dealer quotation system) outside the United States,

   (b) the non-GAAP financial measure is not derived from or based on a measure calculated and presented in accordance with U.S. GAAP, and

   (c) the disclosure is made by the foreign private issuer outside the United States or is in a written communication released only outside the United States.

   This limited exception for foreign private issuers will still apply despite the existence of one or more of the following:

   (i) A written communication is released in the United States as well as outside the United States, so long as the communication is released in the United States contemporaneously with or after the release outside the United States and is not otherwise targeted at persons in the United States.

   (ii) Foreign or U.S. journalists or other third parties have access to the information.

   (iii) The information appears on one or more Web sites of the company, so long as the Web sites are not available exclusively to or targeted at persons located in the United States.

(iv) After its disclosure outside the United States, the information is furnished to the SEC under Form 6-K.

2. For foreign private issuers whose primary financial statements are prepared under home-country GAAP, Regulation G now makes clear that GAAP refers to home-country GAAP. However, if a foreign private issuer includes a non-GAAP financial measure derived from or based on a measure calculated under U.S. GAAP, Regulation G makes it clear that, in such instances, GAAP refers to U.S. GAAP for purposes of applying the requirements of Regulation G to the disclosure of that measure.

3. The SEC also amended annual reports on Form 20-F to incorporate Item 10 of Regulation S-K (as amended). Canadian filers on Form 40-F under the MJDS are not subject to these requirements.

4. Although the requirements apply to annual reports on Form 20-F, a non-GAAP financial measure that would otherwise be prohibited will be permitted in a Form 20-F annual report if the measure is required or expressly permitted under the home-country GAAP used in the issuer's primary financial statements and is included in the issuer's annual report or financial statements used in its home country or market.

5. The rule also does not affect foreign private issuers that file information on Form 6-K.

REAL-TIME DISCLOSURES AND INCREASED SEC REVIEW OF PERIODIC REPORTS

Under Section 409 of the Act, the SEC was authorized but not required to compel companies to make public disclosure on a "rapid and current basis" of additional financial information (i.e., information concerning material changes in financial condition or operations). This authority is in addition to the authority the SEC already has to require current reporting on Form 8-K for U.S. companies and on Form 6-K for non-U.S. companies.

SHORTENED DEADLINES FOR 10-K AND 10-Q

In response to Section 409 of the Act, the SEC adopted final rules that accelerate the filing of periodic reports (i.e., annual reports on Forms 10-K and quarterly reports on Form 10-Q for most U.S. companies eligible to use Form S-3). Additionally, they require those companies to provide additional disclosure about the availability of their periodic and current reports on their Web sites.

The new filing deadlines will be phased in over a three-year period, starting, for most calendar-year companies, with the annual report for the year ended December 31, 2003.

The new rules shorten the deadlines for filing annual reports and quarterly reports for those public companies that are defined as "accelerated filers." After full implementation of the phase-in period, annual reports on Form 10-K will be due 60 days (rather than 90 days) after the end of each fiscal year and quarterly reports on Form 10-Q will be due 35 days (rather than 45 days) after the end of the first, second, and third fiscal quarters.

The SEC deferred implementation of the accelerated reporting regime. For the first fiscal year following adoption of the new rules, the deadlines will remain as they are currently (i.e., 90 days after the end of the fiscal year for Form 10-K and 45 days after the end of the first, second, and third fiscal quarters for Form 10-Q). For the second fiscal year (fiscal years ending on or after December 15, 2003), the deadlines will remain at 45 days after the end of the first, second, and third fiscal quarters for Form 10-Q, but Form 10-K will be due 75 days after the end of the fiscal year. Therefore, for calendar year companies, the initial accelerated filing will be the annual report on Form 10-K for the year ended December 31, 2003. In the third fiscal year (fiscal years ending on or after December 15, 2004), the deadlines will be 60 days for annual reports on Form 10-K and 40 days for quarterly reports on Form 10-Q. Beginning with the fourth fiscal year (fiscal years ending on or after December 15, 2005), the deadline for the Form 10-Q will shorten to 35 days.

The effect of this schedule is that, during each calendar year of the phase-in period, the deadline for the Form 10-K (for the prior fiscal year) and for each Form 10-Q (for the first three quarters in the fiscal year) will shorten by 15 days and five days, respectively. The table below summarizes the filing deadlines for a standard calendar year filer:

| Filing Year | Form 10-K (For Prior Year) | | Form 10-Q | | | |
	Deadline	Date	Deadline	1st Quarter	2nd Quarter	3rd Quarter
2003	90 Days	Mar 31, 2003	45 Days	May 15, 2003	Aug 14, 2003	Nov 14, 2003
2004	75 Days	Mar 15, 2003	40 Days	May 10, 2003	Aug 9, 2003	Nov 9, 2003
2005	60 Days	Mar 1, 2003	35 Days	May 5, 2003	Aug 4, 2003	Nov 5, 2003

Companies having fiscal years ending before December 15 will have more time before the transition than calendar year companies. For example, a November 30 company's first accelerated filing will be its Form 10-K for 2004, due February 14, 2005. A June 30 company's first accelerated filing will be its Form 10-K for its fiscal year ended June 30, 2004, due September 13, 2004.

The rules require accelerated filers to provide disclosures in their annual reports on Form 10-K regarding availability on their Web sites of their periodic and current reports filed with the SEC.

The accelerated filer must disclose its Web site address (URL), if it has one, and it must also disclose whether it makes available free of charge on or though its Web site, if any, its annual report on Form 10-K, quarterly reports on Form 10-Q, current reports on Form 8-K, and all amendments to those reports, with all exhibits and supplemental schedules electronically filed with it, as soon as reasonably practicable after filing or furnishing the material to the SEC.

An accelerated filer that does not make its reports available on its Web site must disclose the reasons for not making its reports available on its Web site and whether it will voluntarily provide electronic or paper copies of such filings free of charge upon request.

The SEC left unchanged the existing reporting deadlines for non-U.S. SEC-reporting companies.

INCREASED SEC REVIEW OF PERIODIC REPORTS

Section 408 of the Act requires the SEC to review a company's Exchange Act reports at least once every three years. For purposes of scheduling these reviews, the SEC is to consider companies in the following categories, among other criteria:

1. Companies that have issued material restatements of financial results,

2. Companies that experience significant volatility in their stock price, as compared with other companies,

3. Companies with the largest market capitalization, and

4. Emerging companies with disparities in price-to-earnings ratios.

The SEC has indicated that it will be developing a selective review approach that uses factors that indicate greater risk of disclosure problems. The SEC has also stated that it will not review every portion of every filing.

CORPORATE GOVERNANCE STANDARDS

The corporate governance standards under the Act focus on the board of directors and its audit committee. As required by Rule 307 of the Act, the SEC adopted a new rule that requires all stock markets to adopt minimum standards under their listing requirements for the composition and functions of audit committees.[1] There are different standards for the independence of audit committee members under SEC Rule 307 and for the independence of directors under the market's listing standards.

THE BOARD OF DIRECTORS

The Act and the SEC implementing rules do not address the role and authority of independent directors, except for the activities of the audit committee. However, the role and authority of the independent directors are addressed by the proposed listing requirements of the NYSE and Nasdaq.

PROPOSED NYSE LISTING REQUIREMENTS

Under the proposed NYSE listing requirements, a majority of the board members must be independent directors. Exempt from this requirement are controlled companies (i.e., where more than 50% of the voting power is held by an individual, a group, or another company), limited partnerships, and companies in bankruptcy.

Independent directors will be required to meet in regularly scheduled executive sessions without management. The name of the director presiding at the executive sessions must be disclosed in the company's proxy statement for its annual meeting or, if the company does not file a proxy statement, in the company's annual report. The proxy statement (or annual report) must also describe how interested parties can communicate with either the presiding director or the independent directors as a group.

Listed companies must have an audit committee, a compensation committee, and a nominating and corporate governance committee, each of which consists entirely of independent directors.

PROPOSED NASDAQ LISTING REQUIREMENTS

Under the proposed Nasdaq listing requirements, a majority of the board members must be independent directors. Exempt from this requirement are controlled companies (i.e., where more than 50% of the voting power is held by an individual, a group, or another company).

Boards must convene regular meetings of the independent directors in executive session.

Companies must have an audit committee composed entirely of independent directors (discussed below).

Listed companies must provide that compensation of the chief executive officer and other executive officers be approved by a compensation committee consisting solely of independent directors or by a majority of all the independent directors, in either case meeting in executive session. (The CEO may be present at meetings concerning the compensation of other executive officers, but may not vote.) However, one non-independent director who is not then an officer or employee or a family member of an officer or employee may serve on a compensation committee of at least three members for up to two years, if the board of directors determines under "exceptional and limited circumstances" that his or her membership is required by the best interests of the company and its shareholders. The nature and reasons for any such board determination of exceptional and limited circumstances must be disclosed in the annual proxy statement.

Listed companies must also provide that director nominations be approved by a nominating committee composed solely of independent directors or by a majority of all the independent directors. However, one non-independent director may serve on the nominating committee of at least three members for up to two years if the director either owns 20% or more of the company's common stock or voting power outstanding (even if he or she is an officer), or is not then an officer or employee or a family member of an officer or employee, and the board of directors determines under "exceptional and limited circumstances" that his or her membership is in the best interest of the company and its shareholders.

DIRECTOR INDEPENDENCE CRITERIA

The Act addresses a director's "independence" only for the audit committee and focuses for these purposes on only two criteria: the acceptance of compensatory fees from the company or any subsidiary (other than for serving as a director) and whether or not the director is an "affiliated person" of the company.

NYSE PROPOSALS

DEFINITION

An "independent director" is one who has no "material relationship" with the listed company. This definition applies for all purposes throughout the NYSE proposals, except that additional restrictions, consistent with Section 301 of the Act, apply to membership on the audit committee.

INDEPENDENCE CRITERIA

For a director to be "independent," the board must affirmatively determine that the director has no "material relationship" with the company either directly or "as a partner, shareholder or officer of an organization that has a relationship with the company." The following relationships presumptively or absolutely disqualify a person from being considered independent.

If a director or a member of his or her immediate family receives direct compensation from the listed company of more than $100,000 per year, excluding director compensation or deferred compensation for prior service, the director is presumptively disqualified. This is a presumption that is rebuttable and can be overcome by the board finding, with unanimous support from the independent directors, that the relationship is not material. However, a current employee of the company can never be deemed independent. If a director or a member of his or her immediate family is affiliated with or employed in a professional capacity by a present or former internal or external auditor of the company, the director is presumptively or absolutely disqualified from being considered independent. If a director or a member of his or her immediate family is employed as an executive officer of a company on the compensation committee of which any executive for the listed company currently serves, the director cannot be considered independent. If a director is an executive officer or an employee or a member of his or her immediate family is an executive officer of another company and either that company accounts for at least 2% of the listed company's consolidated gross revenues or $1 million of such revenues, whichever is greater, or the listed company accounts for at least 2% of that company's consolidated gross revenues or $1 million of such revenues, whichever is greater, the director cannot be considered independent.

Additional independence criteria apply for determining eligibility for audit committee membership.

FIVE-YEAR INDEPENDENCE "COOLING-OFF" PERIOD

In applying the independence criteria discussed above for each specific relationship, a five-year "cooling-off" period is to be applied. No individual can be considered independent who has had such a relationship within the "cooling-off" period or who is a family member of an individual who has had such a relationship within that period, even though that relationship no longer exists. However, during the five years immediately following the effective date of the listing standard, the "look-back" period will extend back only to the effective date of the listing standard.

SHAREHOLDINGS

Ownership of even a significant amount of stock, by itself, is not a bar to independence, because the concern is independence from management. However, shareholding will be relevant to determine a person's status as an "affiliated person" for purposes of applying the independence requirement of the Act for audit committee membership.

OTHER BOARD COMMITTEES

The Act does not address the role or composition of board committees other than the audit committee. However, the role and composition of the board committees other than the audit committee are addressed by the proposed listing requirements of the NYSE and Nasdaq.

NYSE PROPOSALS

NOMINATING AND CORPORATE GOVERNANCE COMMITTEE

The nominating and corporate governance committee composed of independent directors must have a written charter that addresses the committee's purpose. That purpose must include identifying individuals who are qualified to become board members, selecting or recommending that the board select the director nominees for election at the annual meeting of shareholders, and developing and recommending to the board a set of corporate governance principles for the corporation. The committee's goals and responsibilities must reflect the board's criteria for selecting new directors and oversight of the evaluation of the board and management.

The committee must also annually evaluate its performance. Additionally, the charter should give the committee sole authority to hire and fire any search firm used to identify director candidates.

If the company is required by contract or otherwise to provide a third party the ability to nominate one or more directors, the selection of those nominees need not be subject to the nominating committee process.

COMPENSATION COMMITTEE

The compensation committee composed of independent directors must have a written charter that addresses the committee's purpose. That purpose must include discharging the board's responsibilities for compensating the company's executives and producing an annual report on executive compensation for inclusion in the proxy statement of the company's annual meeting in accordance with applicable SEC rules or, if the company does not file a proxy statement, in the company's annual report.

The committee's duties and responsibilities must include reviewing and approving corporate goals and objectives relevant to compensating the chief executive officer, evaluating his or her performance in light of these goals and objectives, having sole authority to determine his or her compensation based on this evaluation, and making recommendations to the board for non-CEO compensation, incentive compensation plans, and equity-based plans.

The committee must also annually evaluate its performance. Additionally, the charter should give the committee sole authority to hire and fire any consulting firm to assist in evaluating the compensation of directors or senior executives, including sole authority to approve the firm's compensation and other retention terms.

NASDAQ PROPOSALS

NOMINATING AND CORPORATE GOVERNANCE COMMITTEE

A nominating committee composed of independent directors must have the authority to nominate individuals for election as directors, unless the independent directors as a group have such authority (except that one member of the nominating committee need not be an independent director in limited and exceptional circumstances). The proposed Nasdaq standards do not require a corporate governance committee.

If a company is required by contract or other lawful arrangement, the provision for nomination of directors by independent means does not apply.

COMPENSATION COMMITTEE

A compensation committee composed of independent directors must have the authority to determine the compensation of all officers, unless the independent directors as a group have such authority (except that one member of the compensation committee need not be an independent director in limited and extraordinary circumstances).

SHAREHOLDER APPROVAL REQUIREMENTS FOR EQUITY COMPENSATION PLANS

The Act does not address shareholder approval requirements for equity compensation plans, but they are addressed by the listing standards of the NYSE and Nasdaq.

NYSE LISTING STANDARDS

Shareholder voting and approval is now required for equity compensation plans. Shareholders must be given the opportunity to vote to approve or disapprove all equity compensation plans, with certain exceptions.

NASDAQ PROPOSALS

Shareholder approval must be obtained for all stock option plans and for any material modification of such plans, with four exceptions: inducement grants to new employees (if such grants are approved by an independent compensation committee or a majority of the independent directors), certain tax-qualified, non-discriminatory employee benefit plans (if such plans are approved by an independent compensation committee or a majority of the independent directors), option plans acquired through mergers, and plans that merely provide a convenient way to purchase shares on the open market or from the company at fair market value.

NOTE

1. Rule 10A-3 under the Exchange Act. Generally, the NYSE corporate governance standards will continue to defer to home-country practices for foreign issuers. However, foreign companies will be required to comply with most of the audit committee requirements (including committee independence, size, and functions).

CHAPTER 7

THE AUDIT COMMITTEE

S ection 301 of the Act directed the SEC to adopt regulations that require the stock exchanges and Nasdaq to prohibit the listing of any security of a company that does not have an audit committee that meets the requirements listed in Section 301. Accordingly, the SEC adopted Rule 10A-3, which requires all U.S. stock exchanges and Nasdaq to adopt listing standards by December 1, 2003 requiring as a minimum condition for original or continued listing of any equity or debt security compliance with the following requirements.

REQUIREMENTS

INDEPENDENCE

Every member of the audit committee of a listed company must be "independent." To be independent, a director may not have accepted any direct or indirect compensation from the company or its subsidiaries, other than compensation for service as a director, and may not be an "affiliated person" of the company. "Affiliated person" means "a person that directly, or indirectly through one or more intermediaries, controls, or is controlled by, or is under common control with, the person specified." The SEC provided a "safe harbor": a person who is not an executive officer of the company or a shareholder owning 10% or more of any class of voting securities of the company would not be deemed to control the listed company.

AUTHORITY AND RESPONSIBILITY

The audit committee must have authority over and be "directly responsible" for hiring, compensating, and retaining the company's independent auditor and for overseeing the work of the auditor in preparing or issuing any audit report (and any related work), including resolving any disagreements between management and the auditor about financial reporting.

The audit committee must establish procedures for receiving, retaining, and treating complaints about accounting, internal controls, or auditing matters and for the confidential, anonymous submission by employees of their concerns about questionable accounting or auditing matters.

The audit committee must have authority to engage independent counsel and other advisors as the committee determines necessary to carry out its duties.

The listed company must provide appropriate funding, as determined by the audit committee, for the compensation of (i) the audit work and any related work of the company's independent auditor, (ii) any other audit, review, or attest services provided to the company by a public accounting firm, and (iii) any advisors engaged by the audit committee.

LISTING STANDARDS AND COMPLIANCE DATES

Rule 10A-3 establishes these as minimum standards for listing; the exchanges and Nasdaq may establish other standards for audit committees and other corporate governance matters that exceed these requirements. The rule does not regulate the size of a listed company's audit committee.

The SEC must approve listing standard amendments sufficient to comply with Rule 10A-3 by December 1, 2003. Listed companies must comply with these standards by the earlier of the listed company's first annual meeting after January 15, 2004 or October 31, 2004.[1]

APPROVAL OF AUDIT ENGAGEMENTS AND OF NON-AUDIT SERVICES TO BE PROVIDED BY AN AUDITOR

The Act requires of every reporting company (even if none of its securities are listed on an exchange or Nasdaq) that the audit committee (or the full board of directors) approve all audit services (including the provision of a comfort letter for a securities offering). Additionally, subject to certain *de minimis* exceptions (i.e. for minor amounts of services), the audit committee (or full board) must approve all permitted non-audit services to be provided by the auditor or its associated persons before the services are provided.

REQUIRED REPORTS TO THE AUDIT COMMITTEE

The Act also requires for any company whose securities trade in the U.S. (even if none of its securities are listed on an exchange or Nasdaq) that the auditor report to the audit committee on a timely basis (i) all critical accounting policies and practices used in the company's audited financial statements, (ii) all alternative treatments of financial information within GAAP that have been discussed with management of the company and the ramifications on the use of such alternative disclosures and treatments and the treatment preferred by the auditor, and (iii) other material written communication between the auditor and the company's management, such as a management letter or schedule of unadjusted differences.

AUDIT COMMITTEE FINANCIAL EXPERT DISCLOSURE

Every company is required to disclose that its board of directors has determined whether or not the company has at least one audit committee financial expert serving on its audit committee and whether or not the audit committee financial expert is "independent."

The company must disclose the name of the audit committee financial expert. A company may, but is not required to, disclose whether it has more than one audit committee financial expert or the names of any additional individuals meeting the criteria. If the company does not have an audit committee financial expert, the company must disclose that and explain why not.

The company must also disclose whether the audit committee financial expert is independent under the listing standards of the AMEX, NYSE, or Nasdaq, as applicable. The full board of directors is required to make the determination that an audit committee member satisfies the criteria for an audit committee financial expert.

REQUIRED ATTRIBUTES

An "audit committee financial expert" must possess all of the following attributes:

❑ An understanding of GAAP and financial statements

❑ The ability to assess the general application of such principles in the accounting for estimates, accruals, and reserves

❑ Experience preparing, auditing, analyzing, or evaluating financial statements that present a complexity of accounting issues that is generally comparable in breadth and level to the complexity of issues that the company's financial statements can reasonably be expected to raise or experience actively supervising one or more persons engaged in such activities

❑ An understanding of internal control for financial reporting

❑ An understanding of audit committee functions

REQUIRED EXPERIENCE

The audit committee financial expert must also have acquired the required attributes through any of the following:

❑ Education and experience as a principal financial officer, principal accounting officer, controller, public accountant, or auditor or experience in one or more positions that involve the performance of similar functions

❑ Experience actively supervising a principal financial officer, principal accounting officer, controller, public accountant, or auditor or person performing similar functions

❏ Experience overseeing or assessing the performance of companies or public accountants for the preparation, auditing, or evaluation of financial statements

❏ Other relevant experience

The audit committee financial expert does not have to have obtained this experience with an SEC reporting company. Experience with private companies that prepare audited financial statements or experience with a foreign company that is not an SEC registrant can also satisfy the requirement.

The board does not have to disclose the basis for the board's determination that the audit committee financial expert has obtained the necessary experience through "other relevant experience." However, the company must briefly list that person's experience in its disclosure. Education alone, without actual experience, would not be considered sufficient.

In addition to having the appropriate knowledge and experience, an audit committee financial expert must possess high standards of personal and professional integrity. Therefore, the board must also consider whether the individual has been subject to any disciplinary actions.

Companies must provide the audit committee financial expert disclosure in their annual reports for fiscal years ending on or after July 15, 2003. For small business issuers, audit committee financial expert disclosure is required for fiscal years ending on or after December 15, 2003.[2]

CODE OF ETHICS FOR SENIOR FINANCIAL OFFICERS AND CHIEF EXECUTIVE OFFICERS

Section 406 of the Act directed the SEC to issue rules requiring a reporting company to disclose whether or not it has a code of ethics for its principal financial officer and controller or principal accounting officer or persons performing similar functions. The SEC included the principal executive officer among those senior managers. The Act also called for requiring companies with no such code of ethics to explain why they have none. The audit committee is often given the responsibility of ensuring compliance with the company's code of ethics.

ATTORNEY REPORTS OF MATERIAL VIOLATIONS

Under the SEC rules implementing Section 307 of the Act, if any attorney representing a reporting company becomes aware of material violations of the securities laws, breaches of fiduciary duty, and similar violations, he or she must report the evidence to the company's chief legal officer. If, then, the company has not provided an appropriate response to the report within a reasonable time, the attorney must report the evidence to the company's audit committee (assuming it has one). If the company then determines that it should assert a defense to any proceeding relating to the evidence (assuming there is a "colorable defense"), the audit committee must approve the retention of counsel who will assert such defense and the chief legal officer must report to the audit committee regularly on the progress of the proceeding. Companies have the option under these regulations to establish, in advance of receiving a report, a "qualified legal compliance committee" of its board of directors to deal with these matters, instead of the audit committee.

NYSE PROPOSALS

INDEPENDENT AUDIT COMMITTEE REQUIRED

For many years, the NYSE has required all listed companies to have an audit committee, consisting of at least three members, all of whom must be independent. The SEC independence standards discussed above (i.e., the independence requirements of Section 301 of the Act and Exchange Act Rule 10A-3(b)(1)) apply for this purpose.

Financial Literacy and Financial Expertise

Audit committee members must be financially literate, as determined by the board, or must become financially literate within a reasonable period of time after their appointment. Additionally, at least one member of the committee (who need not be the committee chair) must have "accounting or related financial management expertise." A board may presume that a person who would be considered an audit committee financial expert under Section 407 of the Act or the related SEC rules has sufficient accounting or related financial management expertise.

Authority over Auditor Relationships

Audit committees must have the sole authority to hire and fire independent auditors and to approve significant non-audit relationships with the independent auditor.

Audit Committee Charter

The audit committee's charter must be in writing and must specify the committee's purpose. That purpose must include assisting board oversight of the integrity of the company's financial statements, the company's compliance with legal and regulatory requirements, the independent auditor's qualifications and independence, and the performance of the company's internal audit function and independent auditors.

The charter must also detail the duties and responsibilities of the audit committee. The charter should cover the following points.

1. The charter should make the audit committee responsible for hiring, retaining, compensating, evaluating, and firing the company's independent auditors, including resolving disagreements between management and the independent auditor and being responsible for the pre-approval of all non-audit services.

2. The charter should establish procedures for the receipt, retention, and treatment of complaints from company employees on accounting, internal accounting controls, or auditing matters,

as well as for the confidential, anonymous submissions by company employees of concerns about questionable accounting or auditing matters.

3. The charter should provide for the audit committee at least annually to obtain and review a report by the independent auditor describing (i) the auditor's internal quality control procedures, (ii) any material issues raised by the auditor's most recent internal quality control review or by its most recent peer review or raised within the preceding five years by any investigation or inquiry by governmental or professional authorities of an independent audit by the firm and any steps taken to deal with these issues, and (iii) all relationships between the independent auditor and the company, in order to assess the auditor's independence.

4. The charter should provide for the committee to discuss the annual audited financial statement and quarterly financial statements with management and the independent auditor and the company's disclosure in the related MD&A sections as well as earnings press releases and financial information and earnings guidance that are given to analysts and rating agencies.

5. The charter should give the committee the authority to obtain the advice and assistance of outside legal, accounting or other advisors, as appropriate.

6. The charter should provide for the audit committee to receive from the company the funds it determines necessary to compensate the outside legal, accounting, or other advisors employed by the audit committee.

7. The charter should give the committee authority and responsibility for discussing policies for risk assessment and risk management.

8. The charter should provide for the committee to meet separately, periodically, with management, with the internal auditors, and with the independent auditors as well as review with the independent auditor any audit problems or difficulties and management's response.

9. The charter should set clear hiring policies for employees or former employees of the independent auditor.

10. The charter should provide for the committee to report regularly to the board on any issues that arise within its oversight responsibilities.

In addition, the audit committee is responsible for preparing the report that is required to be included in the company's annual proxy statement or, if the company does not file a proxy statement, in the company's annual report. Finally, it must also annually assess the sufficiency of its charter and annually evaluate the performance of its responsibilities.

NASDAQ PROPOSALS

INDEPENDENT AUDIT COMMITTEE REQUIRED

As Nasdaq has required for years, all listed companies must have an audit committee, consisting of at least three members, all of whom must be independent. Nasdaq's proposed independence standards, discussed above, will apply to determine audit committee eligibility. However, one member need not meet those standards if the board of directors has determined under "exceptional and limited circumstances" that such individual's membership is required by the best interest of the company and its shareholders and he meets certain other criteria. The board must disclose in the proxy statement for the next annual meeting after that determination the nature of the relationship and the reasons for the determination. However, a member appointed on such an exceptional basis may not serve longer than two years and may not chair the committee.

ADDITIONAL INDEPENDENCE REQUIREMENTS FOR AUDIT COMMITTEE MEMBERS

An audit committee member must meet the independence requirements of Section 301 of the Act and Exchange Act Rule 10A-3(b)(1) and may not own or control 10% or more of the company's voting securities.

FINANCIAL LITERACY

Audit committee members must be able to read and understand financial statements when they are appointed. Additionally, at least one member of the committee will be required to have had past employment experience in finance or accounting, professional certification in accounting, or other comparable experience or background that qualifies him or her as financially sophisticate, such as being or having been a chief executive officer, chief financial officer, or other senior official with financial oversight responsibilities.

AUTHORITY OVER AUDITOR RELATIONSHIPS

Audit committees must have the sole authority to hire, determine compensation for, and oversee the independent auditor and must approve, in advance, all audit and permissible non-audit services. Audit committees must also have authority to engage and determine funding for independent counsel and other advisors and to establish procedures for complaints about the company's financial report as provided by the Act.

AUDIT COMMITTEE RESPONSIBILITIES AND CHARTER

The audit committee charter must be in writing and must specify the scope of the committee's responsibilities (including structure, processes, and membership requirements) and specify the committee's responsibility for ensuring the receipt from the independent auditor of a formal, written statement delineating all relationships between the auditor and the company. It must be consistent with auditor professional responsibility standards (Independence Standards Board No. 1). It must specify the committee's responsibility for actively engaging in a dialogue with the auditor concerning disclosed relationships or services that may affect the objectivity and independence of the auditor and for taking, or recommending that the board take, appropriate action to oversee the independence of the auditor.

The audit committee must also specify its authority and responsibility, as provided by the Act, for overseeing the accounting and financial reporting processes and the audits of the financial statement of the company, hiring, determining the funding for and overseeing the outside auditors, pre-approving all audit and permissible non-audit services, establishing procedures for receipt of complaints regarding the company's financial reporting and internal controls, and engaging and determining funding for independent counsel and other advisors to the committee. The committee must also assess annually the sufficiency of its charter.

RELATED PARTY/CONFLICT OF INTEREST TRANSACTIONS

All related party transactions must be approved by the audit committee (or a comparable independent body of the board) as part of the company's obligation to conduct an "appropriate review ... on an ongoing basis" of such transactions. "Related party transactions" are transactions that are required to be disclosed under SEC rules. For a body to be considered "comparable" to the audit committee, all directors of the body that review and approve a related party transaction must be both independent under Nasdaq rules and also disinterested in the transaction.

NOTES

1. Foreign private issuers and small business issuers will have until July 31, 2005 to comply.
2. Like U.S. companies, foreign private issuers must disclose whether or not they have an audit committee financial expert. However, non-U.S. companies do not have to disclose whether the expert is independent until July 31, 2005.

CHAPTER 8

CODES OF CONDUCT AND ETHICS, GOVERNANCE GUIDELINES

SARBANES-OXLEY ACT AND SEC IMPLEMENTING RULES

FINANCIAL OFFICERS CODE OF ETHICS

Under Section 406 of the Act, the SEC has adopted rules requiring all reporting companies (including non-U.S. companies), to disclose whether the company has adopted a written code of ethics for the company's principal executive officer, principal financial officer, principal accounting officer or controller, or persons performing similar functions.

The rules do not require a company to adopt a code of ethics if it has not already done so or to amend an existing code of ethics. However, a company that does not have a code of ethics must explain why it does not have such a code. If a company has a defective code, i.e., one that does not satisfy all the requirements of the rule, the company may not affirm that it has the required code.

Companies must provide code of ethics disclosure in their annual reports for fiscal years ending on or after July 15, 2003, except for small business issuers, which will be required to include such disclosure for fiscal years ending on or after December 15, 2003. Thereafter, companies must comply with the disclosure requirements for amendments or waivers to their codes of ethics.

CONTENTS OF THE CODE OF ETHICS

Under Section 406, a code of ethics means standards that are reasonably designed to deter wrongdoing and to promote the following:

1. Honest and ethical conduct, including ethical handling of actual or apparent conflicts of interest between personal and professional relationships;

2. Full, fair, accurate, timely, and understandable disclosure in reports and documents that a company files with or submits to the SEC and in provides in other public communications;

3. Compliance with applicable laws, rules, and regulations;

4. Prompt internal reporting to an appropriate person identified in the code of violations of the code; and

5. Accountability for adherence to the code.

A company may have different codes of ethics for different types of officers and the required code may be part of a broader code that addresses additional issues and applies to additional persons. Codes of ethics vary from company to company; decisions as to the specific provisions of a company's code, compliance procedures, and disciplinary measures for breaches of the code remain with the company. The SEC has strongly encouraged companies to adopt codes that are broader and more comprehensive than necessary to meet the disclosure requirements.

MAKING CODES PUBLICLY AVAILABLE

The rules provide for the following three methods of making a company's code publicly available:

❏ Filing it as an exhibit to the company's annual report

❏ Posting it (or relevant portions) on its Web site, provided that the company has disclosed its Internet address in its applicable annual report

❏ Offering in its annual report to provide a copy to any person without charge on request

If the company includes its Web site address in its annual report, that would not, by itself, include or incorporate by reference all the information on the company's Web site into the annual report (with the resulting liability), unless the company otherwise acts to incorporate such information. If a company has multiple Web sites that it uses for various purposes, such as investor relations, product information, and business-to-business activities, the disclosure requirement would require the company to post the code of ethics on the Web site it normally uses for investor relations.

Disclosure of Changes or Waivers of an Ethics Code Provision

All companies must disclose either an amendment to any provision of a company's code of ethics that applies to the specified officers or a waiver (including an implicit waiver) of an ethics code provision to a specified officer, the name of the person to whom the waiver was granted, and the date of the waiver. If a company has a broad-based code of ethics that covers more than the senior officers, a change or waiver of a provision that relates to other officers or to the directors of the company would not require disclosure.

NYSE PROPOSALS

Code of Business Conduct and Ethics

Companies are required to adopt and disclose a Code of Business Conduct and Ethics for directors, officers, and employees that addresses conflicts of interest, corporate opportunities, confidentiality, fair dealing, protection and proper use of company assets, compliance with laws, rules and regulations (including insider trading laws), and encouraging the reporting of any illegal or unethical behavior.

Companies must promptly disclose any waivers under the Code of Business Conduct and Ethics given to directors and officers.

Corporate Governance Guidelines

The NYSE requires companies to adopt and disclose corporate governance guidelines, which must address:

- ❏ Director qualification standards
- ❏ Director responsibilities
- ❏ Director access to management and, as necessary and appropriate, to independent advisors
- ❏ Director compensation
- ❏ Director orientation and continuing education
- ❏ Management succession
- ❏ An annual self-evaluation of the board's performance.

NASDAQ PROPOSALS

CODE OF CONDUCT

Companies must adopt a code of conduct for all directors, officers, and employees that is publicly available and includes the elements necessary to meet the code of ethics requirements established by the SEC under Section 406 of the Act. Additionally, the code must provide for an enforcement mechanism.

Companies must disclose any waivers given to executive officers and directors and the waivers must be approved by the board or a board committee.

EDUCATION AND TRAINING OF DIRECTORS

The Act and SEC implementing rules do not address education and training of directors. However, both the NYSE and Nasdaq have established requirements in this area.

The corporate governance guidelines for NYSE will require companies to address the continuing education and training of directors. The NYSE has indicated that it intends to help develop and sponsor appropriate education and training programs. In contrast, Nasdaq will require that directors of listed companies undertake continuing education under rules to be developed by the Nasdaq Listing and Hearing Review Council and approved by the Nasdaq Board.

OTHER STANDARDS APPLICABLE TO DIRECTORS OR OFFICERS

PROHIBITION ON PERSONAL LOANS

Reporting companies are prohibited under Section 402 of the Act from extending, maintaining, or arranging for personal loans to their directors or executives. Excluded from this prohibition are certain consumer credit arrangements (such as home improvement or credit card loans) made in the ordinary course of business, of a type generally made available by the company to the public, and on market terms no more favorable than those offered by the company to the general public. For example, companies that are or own securities brokerage firms may make margin loans to employees, unless used to carry stock of the company. Personal loans already in existence when the Act became effective on July 30, 2002 may continue in effect, provided there is no material modification to any term or any renewal of the loan after that date.

REPORTING INSIDER TRADING

Under Section 403 of the Act, the SEC adopted new rules implementing changes to Section 16(a) of the Exchange Act. Under Section 16(a) and related SEC rules, officers, directors, and 10% shareholders of equity securities of a reporting company must file reports with the SEC describing their ownership and trades in the company's equity securities.[1] Under the new rules, the reports must be filed on an accelerated basis, generally within two business days of the trade or other event triggering the filing.

The SEC also adopted rules mandating the electronic filing of all Section 16 reports (i.e., Forms 3, 4, and 5) on the SEC's EDGAR system.

The new rules also require a company that maintains a corporate Web site to post on its Web site all Section 16 reports filed by its insiders by the end of the business day (i.e., 10 p.m., Eastern time) after filing any such report. Postings on a company's Web site must remain accessible for at least 12 months.

INSIDER TRADING DURING PENSION FUND BLACKOUT PERIODS

Under Section 306(a) of the Act, the SEC adopted new rules regulating securities trades by insiders during pension fund blackout periods. The new rules are entitled Regulation Blackout Trading Restriction ("Regulation BTR").

Section 306(a) of the Act and the related SEC rules are intended to prevent directors and executive officers from selling their equity securities when other employees (or a substantial number of them) cannot. Section 306(a) of the Act prohibits executive officers and directors, during any blackout period, from acquiring any equity securities in connection with service or employment as a director or executive officer and from disposing of any equity securities previously acquired in connection with service or employment as a director or executive officer. Section 306(a) and Regulation BTR apply to all reporting companies.[2]

Under Regulation BTR, there is a rebuttable presumption that any equity securities sold or otherwise transferred during a blackout period by a director or executive officer were acquired in connection with service or employment as a director or executive officer to the extent that he or she holds such securities.

TRANSACTIONS EXEMPT FROM TRADING PROHIBITION

Regulation BTR provides exemptions from the blackout trading prohibition for the following transactions in a company's equity securities:

1. acquisitions under broad-based, nondiscriminatory dividend or interest reinvestment plans;

2. purchases or sales under Rule 10b5-1 trading arrangements, provided that the arrangement is not entered into or modified during the blackout period;

3. increases or decreases due to stock splits or stock dividends that apply equally to all securities of that class or from the exercise of rights granted pro rata to all holders of the same class of securities;

4. purchases or sales under tax conditioned plans (e.g., stock purchase plans and excess benefit plans) under the Internal Revenue Code, but not "discretionary transactions" involving such plans (such as an intra-fund transfers);

5. compensatory grants and awards (including options and stock appreciation rights) under a plan that provides for automatic grants or awards to directors or executive officers and specifies the terms and conditions of the grants or awards; and

6. certain exercises, conversions, or terminations of derivative securities that were not written or acquired during the relevant blackout period and where the security may be exercised, converted, or terminated only on a fixed date or the security is exercised, converted, or terminated by a counterparty free from influence by the director or executive officer.

Generally, Regulation BTR also exempts transactions that occur automatically or otherwise outside the control of the officer or director.

BLACKOUT PERIOD

"Blackout period" means any period of more than three consecutive business days during which the ability of at least 50% of the participants or beneficiaries under all individual account plans of the company to purchase, sell, or otherwise acquire or transfer an interest in any equity security of the company held in such an individual account plan is temporarily suspended by the company or by a fiduciary of the plan.

A company must timely notify its directors and executive officers and the SEC of the imposition of a blackout period that would trigger the statutory trading prohibition.

FORFEITURE OF CERTAIN BONUSES AND PROFITS

Section 304 of the Act provides that if a company must restate its financial statements as a result of "misconduct," the company's CEO and CFO must disgorge to the company (i) any bonus or other incentive-based or equity-based compensation received during the 12-month period following the issuance or filing with the SEC (whichever is earlier) of a financial document embodying the financial reporting requirement and (ii) any profits from the sale of the company's securities during the 12-month period. Section 304 applies to U.S. and non-U.S. reporting companies.[3]

Section 304 raises many questions for which there generally are no clear answers. For example, the statute does not define what constitutes "misconduct" nor does it require that the CEO or CFO be the source of the misconduct. Further, it may often be unclear as to when, for purposes of Section 304, an officer receives certain compensation (e.g., options subject to multi-year vesting schedules) or how the profits subject to disgorgement are to be measured.

IMPROPER INFLUENCE ON CONDUCT OF AUDITS

The SEC adopted rules to implement Section 303(a) of the Act.[4] The new rule prohibits officers and directors or those acting under their direction from coercing, manipulating, misleading, or fraudulently influencing any auditor engaged in the performance of an audit of the company's financial statements, if such person knew or should have known that the action could render the financial statements misleading.

The phrase "engaged in the performance of an audit" should be read broadly to encompass the "professional engagement" period and any other time the auditor is called upon to make decisions or judgments regarding the company's financial statements. Consequently, the rule could apply after the engagement period has ended, for example, when the auditor is asked to consent to use, reissuance, or withdrawal of a prior report. Similarly, action taken before the engagement period begins—for example, if retention of the auditor is made contingent upon the auditor agreeing to issue an unwarranted, unqualified audit opinion or to limit the scope of the audit—could also violate the rule. Further, the rule is not limited to the audit of the annual financial statements, but applies to related activities (for example, improperly influencing an auditor during a review of interim financial statements) that the SEC believes are sufficiently connected to the harm the Act is intended to prevent.

TEMPORARY FREEZE AUTHORITY FOR THE SEC

Section 1103 of the Act amended Section 21C(c) of the Exchange Act to provide that if, during an investigation involving possible violations of the federal securities laws by a public company or any of its directors, officers, partners, controlling persons, agents, or employees, it appears likely to the SEC that the company will make extraordinary payments to any of those persons, the SEC may petition a federal district court for a temporary order requiring the company to escrow those payments in an interest-bearing account for 45 days subject to court supervision. Besides providing that the "extraordinary payments" may be "compensation or otherwise," the statute does not define the term. The company must receive notice and have an opportunity to be heard before an order may be entered, unless the court decides that to do so would be impracticable or contrary to the public interest.

In apparently the first exercise of this new authority by the SEC, on May 13, 2003 the U.S. District Court for the Central District of

California granted the SEC's request for a temporary order placing in escrow $37.64 million in cash payments that Gemstar-TV Guide International, Inc. had previously agreed to make to its former chief executive officer and chief financial officer.

NOTES

1. Section 16(a) and thus the new SEC rules apply only to U.S. companies. Insiders of non-U.S. companies are not subject to the Section 16(a) filing requirements.
2. Directors and executive officers of U.S. companies, non-U.S. companies, small business issuers, and, in limited circumstances, registered investment companies are subject to the trading prohibition. However, Regulation BTR limits Section 306(a)'s application to non-U.S. companies to where 50% or more of the U.S. participants are "blacked out" and they represent an appreciable portion of the companies' employees worldwide.
3. Application of these provisions to non-U.S. companies may be problematic if any required repayment would violate the employment laws of a non-U.S. jurisdiction.
4. Rule 13b2-2(b)(1).

AUDITOR INDEPENDENCE

Under Section 208(a) of the Act, the SEC has adopted new rules that expand the requirements for auditor independence. The rules address "cooling off" after employment relationships, scope of services provided by independent auditors, mandatory rotation of audit partners, and other matters regarding auditor independence.

The rules apply to auditors, including foreign accounting firms, of reporting companies (U.S. and non-U.S.). Although the rules became effective on May 6, 2003, they contain various transition periods.

"COOLING OFF" AFTER EMPLOYMENT RELATIONSHIPS

THE NEW RULES

Under the new rules, an accounting firm will not be independent if an employee of the company with a "financial reporting oversight role" was a member of the accounting firm's audit engagement team at any time within the one-year period (the "cooling-off period") preceding the start of audit procedures for the current year.

Employees subject to the cooling-off period are the chief executive officer, the chief financial officer, the controller, the chief accounting officer (or any person serving in any equivalent position), every individual in a financial reporting oversight role (i.e., any role in which a person is in a position to influence the contents of financial statements), or anyone who prepares financial statements.

Members of the engagement team are the lead audit partner, the concurring audit partner, and any individual who provides more than 10 hours of audit, review, or attest services during the annual audit period.

CALCULATING THE ONE-YEAR COOLING-OFF PERIOD

Audit procedures are deemed to have commenced for the current audit engagement period the day after the company's prior year's annual report is filed with the SEC and to end on the date the current year's annual report is filed. For example, if a calendar-year reporting company files its Form 10-K on March 15, 2003, April 5, 2004, and March 10, 2005, the 2003 audit engagement period will commence on March 16, 2003 and will end on April 5, 2004, while the 2004 audit engagement period will commence on April 6, 2004 and end on March 10, 2005.

If an engagement team member provides audit, review, or attest services for a company at any time during the 2003 engagement period (March 16, 2003-April 5, 2004) and he or she begins employment with the company in a financial reporting oversight role before March 10, 2005, the accounting firm would be deemed to be not independent of the company. Thus, the new rules require the accounting firm to complete one annual audit after the individual was a member of the audit engagement team.

SCOPE OF SERVICES PROVIDED BY AUDITORS

INTRODUCTION

Under the Act it is unlawful for a registered public accounting firm that performs an audit for a company to contemporaneously provide the company with nine categories of non-audit services. The auditor may provide other non-audit services that are permitted, including tax services, if they are approved in advance by the company's audit committee.

The SEC rules further describe the non-audit services prohibited under the Act. Only non-audit services to audit clients are prohibited. The rules do not apply to services provided to non-audit clients.

PROHIBITED SERVICES SUBSTANTIALLY UNCHANGED BY THE NEW RULES

The new rules for the following three non-audit services are substantially identical to the SEC's previous prohibitions.

MANAGEMENT FUNCTIONS. The rules prohibit an auditor from acting as a director, officer, or employee of an audit client or from performing any decision-making, supervisory, or ongoing monitoring function for an audit client. However, auditors may continue to evaluate an audit client's internal controls and to recommend improvements to the design and implementation of internal controls and risk management controls.

HUMAN RESOURCES. Auditors may not conduct human resource functions for audit clients, including job searches for executive or managerial positions, psychological or other testing of potential employees, reference or background checks, negotiating terms of employment, and recommending or advising the hiring of specific job candidates.

BROKER-DEALER, INVESTMENT ADVISOR, OR INVESTMENT BANKING SERVICES. An auditor may not act as a broker-dealer (registered or unregistered), promoter, or underwriter for an audit client; make investment decisions for the audit client; or otherwise have discretionary authority over an audit client's investments. Auditors are also prohibited from executing transactions for an audit client or having custody of an audit client's assets.

PROHIBITED SERVICES EXPANDED BY THE NEW RULES

The new rules broaden the existing prohibitions (i.e., remove exceptions) against providing the following services.

BOOKKEEPING OR OTHER SERVICES RELATED TO ACCOUNTING RECORDS OR FINANCIAL STATEMENTS. Providing any bookkeeping services for an audit client will impair auditor independence unless it is reasonable to conclude that the results of these services will not be subject to audit procedures during an audit of the client's financial statements. Bookkeeping services include maintaining or preparing the audit client's accounting records, preparing financial statements that are filed with the SEC or the information that forms the basis of financial statements filed with the SEC, or preparing or originating source data underlying the audit client's financial statements.[1]

FINANCIAL INFORMATION SYSTEMS DESIGN AND IMPLEMENTATION. Auditors may not provide any service related to an audit client's financial information systems design and implementation, unless it is reasonable to conclude that the results of these services will not be subject to audit procedures during an audit of the client's financial statements. Auditors may continue to evaluate and make recommendations to audit clients on internal controls.

APPRAISAL OR VALUATION SERVICES, FAIRNESS OPINIONS, OR CONTRIBUTION-IN-KIND REPORTS. The rules prohibit an auditor from providing any appraisal service, any valuation service, or any service involving a fairness opinion or contribution-in-kind report for an audit client, unless it is reasonable to conclude that the results of these services will not be subject to audit procedures during an audit of the client's financial statements.

ACTUARIAL SERVICES. Auditors may not provide any actuarially oriented advisory service involving the determination of amounts recorded in an audit client's financial statements and related accounts, unless it is reasonable to conclude that the results of these services will not be subject to audit procedures during an audit of the audit client's financial statements. However, auditors may assist a client in understanding the methods, models, assumptions, and inputs used in computing such amounts.

INTERNAL AUDIT OUTSOURCING. The rules prohibit auditors from providing any internal audit service that has been outsourced by the audit client that relates to the audit client's internal accounting controls, financial systems, or financial statements, unless it is reasonable to conclude that the results of these services will not be subject to audit procedures during an audit of the client's financial statements.

LEGAL SERVICES. Under the rules, an auditor may not provide an audit client with any service that, under the circumstances, could be provided only by someone licensed or otherwise qualified to practice law where the service is provided.[2]

EXPERT SERVICES. The Act added "expert services" as a prohibited non-audit service. Auditors are prohibited from providing expert opinions or other services to an audit client or its legal representative in litigation or in regulatory or administrative investigations or proceedings. For example, this includes forensic accounting services provided to the audit client's attorneys for the defense of an SEC investigation. However, an auditor may perform internal investigations or fact-finding engagements for audit clients and may testify or otherwise provide factual accounts in investigations or proceedings regarding any services provided to the audit client.

TAX SERVICES. An auditor may provide tax services to its audit clients without impairing its independence. Auditors may continue to provide tax compliance, tax planning, and tax advice to audit clients, subject to the normal audit committee pre-approval requirements. The new rules also require companies to disclose in annual reports and proxy statements the amount of fees paid to auditors for tax services. Additionally, the audit committee should scrutinize carefully the retention of an accountant in tax avoidance transactions recommended by the accountant that may not be supported by tax law.

PARTNER ROTATION

The new SEC rules require the lead and concurring partners to rotate off the client after five years and be subject to a five-year "time-out" period. Audit partners, other than the lead and concurring partners, must rotate off after no more than seven years and are subject to a two-year time-out. In this way, a partner could serve either as the lead partner on a significant subsidiary or as an "audit partner" at the parent or issuer level for up to two years before becoming the lead or concurring partner on the engagement and still be able to serve in that lead or concurring role for five years.

The rules apply the partner rotation requirements to "audit partners." In addition to the lead and concurring partners, "audit partners" include partners on the audit engagement team who have responsibility for decision-making on significant auditing, accounting, and reporting matters that affect the financial statements or who maintain regular contact with management and the audit committee. In particular, audit partners would include all those who serve the client at the issuer or parent level. Further, the definition of "audit partner" includes the lead partner on subsidiaries of the company whose assets or revenues constitute 20% or more of the consolidated assets or revenues. However, "specialty" and "national office" partners are not "audit partners."

AUDIT COMMITTEE OVERSIGHT OF THE ENGAGEMENT

The rules require the audit committee to approve in advance all audit, review, and attest services and all permitted non-audit services. An auditor will not be deemed independent for an engagement unless the engagement of the auditor is approved in advance by the company's committee or by one or more board members who are independent directors and who are designated to perform this role or under all three of the following conditions:

1. The engagement is entered into under policies for pre-approval and detailed procedures that are established by the audit committee for the particular service and that are designed to safeguard the independence of the auditor.

2. The audit committee is informed promptly of each engagement.

3. The policies and procedures do not include delegating the audit committee's responsibilities to management.

The Act provides a *de minimis* (i.e., for minor amounts) exception from the pre-approval requirements for the provision of non-audit services where all the services do not aggregate more than 5% of total revenues paid by the audit client to its accountant in the fiscal year in which the services are provided, the services were not recognized as non-audit services at the time of the engagement, and the services are promptly brought to the attention of the audit committee and approved before the completion of the audit either by the audit committee or by one or more members of the audit committee to whom authority to grant such approvals was delegated.

The rules view "audit services" as broader than those services generally required for an audit under GAAP. For example, audit services include comfort letters and statutory audits for insurance companies. Audit services would also include services performed to fulfill the accountants' responsibility under GAAP. For example, a tax partner may need to review the tax account in the financial statements as a part of the audit process.

These rules apply to all audit services(including review and attest) and permitted non-audit services that are contracted for on or after May 6, 2003. For arrangements for non-audit services entered into before that date (whether or not they were pre-approved by the audit committee), the accounting firm will have until May 6, 2004 to complete those services.

COMMUNICATION WITH THE AUDIT COMMITTEES

Each auditor that performs any audit required under the securities laws must report to the audit committee before the filing of its audit report with the SEC:

1. All critical accounting policies and practices to be used (critical accounting policies are discussed earlier)

2. All alternative treatments within GAAP for policies and practices related to material items that have been discussed with management, including the ramifications of the use of such alternative disclosures and treatments and the treatment preferred by the registered public accounting firm

3. Other material written communications between auditor and management, such as any management letter or schedule of unadjusted differences

The communications concerning general accounting policies should focus on the initial selection and changes in significant accounting policies. The communications should include the effect of management's judgments and accounting estimates, as well as the auditor's judgments about the quality of the entity's accounting principles. The discussion of general accounting policies should include the range of alternatives available under GAAP that were discussed by management and the auditors as well as the reasons why the chosen policy was selected. If an existing accounting policy is being modified, then the auditor should describe the reasons for the change. Whenever a new accounting policy or treatment selected is not the auditor's preferred policy or treatment, the discussions should include the reasons why the auditor considered one policy or treatment to be preferable but management did not select that policy or treatment.

OTHER MATERIAL COMMUNICATIONS

The rules require auditors to provide the audit committee with copies of material written communications between the auditor and management. Some communications that will be considered material to a company include management representation letters, reports on observations and recommendations on internal controls, schedules of unadjusted audit differences and a listing of adjustments and reclassifications not recorded, engagement letters, and letters confirming the auditor's independence.

Auditors should consider carefully what other written communications should be provided to audit committees.

TIMING OF COMMUNICATIONS

Communications between an auditor and the audit committee must occur before the filing of an audit report with the SEC, including before the filing of annual reports and proxy statements, registration statements, and other periodic or current reports that contain audit reports.

EXPANDED DISCLOSURE

The rules require a company to disclose the following information about its "principal accountant" in its annual and proxy statement.[3]

❑ The aggregate "Audit Fees" billed for each of the last two fiscal years for the audit and quarterly reviews or services that are normally provided by the accountant for statutory and regulatory filings or engagements. (This includes all services performed to comply with GAAP, which might include certain tax and accounting services and related services that only the independent accountant reasonably can provide, such as comfort letters.)

❑ The aggregate "Audit-Related Fees billed in each of the last two years that are reasonably related to the audit or review." (This includes assurance and related services such as due diligence and internal control reviews. The nature of the services must also be described.)

❑ The aggregate "Tax Fees" billed in each of the last two years for tax compliance, tax advice, and tax planning (together with a description of the nature of the services).

❑ The aggregate amount of "All Other Fees" billed in each of the last two fiscal years (together with a description of the nature of the services).

❑ The audit committee's pre-approval policies and procedures.

❑ The percentage of "Audit-Related Fees, Tax Fees and All Other Fees" that were approved by the audit committee under the *de minimis* exception.

❑ If more than 50%, the percentage of hours expended on the principal accountant's engagement to audit the annual financial statements that were attributable to work performed by part-time, temporary employees.

These disclosure provisions are effective for periodic annual filings for the first fiscal year ending after December 15, 2003.

COMPENSATION

The rule prohibits auditors from setting an audit partner's compensation or allocation of partnership "units" based on the sale of non-audit services to clients. An auditor is not independent under the rules if, at any time during the audit engagement period, any "audit partner" receives compensation based on the partner's procuring engagements from the client to provide any services that are not audit, review, or attest services.

The restriction applies during the "audit and professional engagement period," which begins when the auditor signs an initial engagement letter or begins audit, review, or attest procedures and ends when the client or auditor notifies the SEC that the client is no longer the auditor's client.

The term "audit partner" refers to the lead and concurring partners and other partners on the engagement team who are responsible for making decisions on significant auditing, accounting, and reporting matters affecting the financial statements or who maintain regular contact with management or the audit committee. The restriction does not apply to specialty partners such as tax and valuation specialists, even if they are consulted during the audit engagement.

Notes

1. Similarly, an auditor that prepares statutory financial statements for a non-U.S. company would not be independent if those statements form the basis of financial statements filed with the SEC.
2. In some non-U.S. jurisdictions, tax work may be performed only by someone licensed to practice law; an accounting firm providing such service would therefore be deemed to be providing prohibited legal services. The new rules are not intended to prevent foreign accountants from providing services that U.S. auditors may provide; in determining whether auditor independence is impaired, the SEC will look to whether providing the service would be prohibited in the U.S. as well as the foreign jurisdiction. The SEC encouraged foreign accountants and regulators to consult with the SEC staff to address these issues.
3. This includes on annual report on Form 20-F for foreign private issuers or Form 40-F for Canadian companies.

CHAPTER 11

OVERSIGHT BOARD AND REGULATION

Title I of the Act covers the establishment and organization of the Public Company Accounting Oversight Board (PCAOB).

ESTABLISHMENT AND ADMINISTRATIVE PROCEDURES

Section 101 establishes an independent, non-governmental board to oversee the audits of public companies to protect the interests of investors and to further public confidence in independent audit reports. The powers of the PCAOB are as follows:

- To register and discipline accounting firms that audit public companies;

- To establish audit and accounting standards; and

- To investigate financial irregularities.

The following PCAOB inaugural members were appointed:

- William McDonough (designated Chairman)

- Kayla J. Gillan

- Daniel L. Goelzer

- Willis D. Gradison, Jr.

- Charles D. Niemeier

The PCAOB has three main divisions:

- Auditing standards
- Registration and inspection
- Enforcement

The administrative staff of the PCAOB consists of the following positions:

- Chief of Staff
- Chief Auditor
- Deputy Chief Auditor
- Director, Registration and Inspections
- Acting General Counsel
- Director, Human Resources
- Chief Administrative Officer
- Chief Information Officer
- Director, Public Affairs
- Director, Government Relations

REGISTRATION WITH THE BOARD

Section 102 requires public accounting firms to register with the Board and take certain other actions to perform audits of companies.[1] The registration applications must be filed electronically. They are quite extensive and are public documents, but confidentiality may be granted for parts upon request. The Board has discretion to reject applications. There is an application fee, which is intended to cover the cost of processing the application. Last, registered firms must submit an annual report to the PCAOB.

AUDITING, QUALITY CONTROL, AND INDEPENDENCE STANDARDS AND RULES

Section 103 requires the PCAOB to establish, through the adoption of standards proposed by one or more professional groups of accountants, auditing standards and related attestation standards for registered public accounting firms to use in preparing and issuing audit reports. The Act gives the PCAOB the power to establish both auditing and accounting standards. The current plans are to leave the establishment of accounting standards to the FASB. While the PCAOB will set its own audit standards, it has temporarily adopted the current Accounting Principles Board (APB) standards. The independence standards are within auditing standards.

INSPECTIONS OF REGISTERED PUBLIC ACCOUNTING FIRMS

Section 104 requires the PCAOB to conduct a continuing program of inspections to assess the degree of compliance of each registered public accounting firm with the Act. The inspection program is expected to be a major focus of the Board. National firms are to be inspected annually, with Big Four inspections to start in 2003. Other registered firms are to be inspected every three years. The inspections are likely to be modeled on the AICPA peer review program, with various enhancements. Documents and testimony obtained in the inspection process will be confidential, but inspection reports will likely be public documents. Unsatisfactory inspections may be referred to disciplinary staff.

INVESTIGATIONS AND DISCIPLINARY PROCEEDINGS

Section 105 requires the PCAOB to establish rules and procedures for the investigation and disciplining of registered public accounting firms.

The PCAOB has broad powers to investigate financial frauds. Emergency response team inspections and traditional investigations may be conducted by staff without Board approval and investigations may be formal as well as informal. The PCAOB can compel registered firms and public companies to comply with its requests. The sanctions for failure to comply consist of the suspension or revocation of an accounting firm's registration and the PCAOB may seek an SEC subpoena for public companies. The PCAOB's greater accounting resources will make such investigations quite formidable. However, the SEC is to receive notice of all PCAOB investigations.

FOREIGN PUBLIC ACCOUNTING FIRMS

Section 106 requires that any foreign public accounting firm that prepares or furnishes an audit report for any company shall be subject to the Act, in the same manner and to the same extent as a U.S. public accounting firm, except that registration does not by itself provide a basis for subjecting the foreign public accounting firm to the jurisdiction of a U.S. court.

SEC OVERSIGHT, ACCOUNTING STANDARDS, AND FUNDING

Section 107 states that the SEC shall have oversight and enforcement authority over the PCAOB. Section 108 amends Section 19 of the Securities Act in that the SEC may recognize under Section 13(b) of the Exchange Act as "generally accepted" any accounting principles established by a standard-setting body that meets certain criteria, as further specified in the Act. Those powers have been delegated by the SEC to the FASB for now.

Section 109 provides for funding of the PCAOB, which is to be done by assessments, largely on public companies and to a lesser extent on registered accounting firms. The amount each company will be assessed depends on the market capitalization of the company. Companies with under a $25 million market capitalization will not be assessed. The failure to pay the assessment will lead to a "no audit opinion" and a stop-trading order. Registered accounting firms will pay an annual registration fee.

EFFECTIVE DATE AND TRANSITION

The SEC determined as of April 25, 2003 that the Board was properly organized and had the capacity to carry out the requirements of the Act. Public accounting firms then had 180 days to register with the Board (i.e., no later than October 22, 2003). Foreign accounting firms have an extra six months to comply.

Notes

1. There is no exemption for non-U.S. public accounting firms, but they have a six-month extension.

ATTORNEY PROFESSIONAL RESPONSIBILITY (SECTION 307)

The SEC has adopted new rules under Section 307 of the Act for minimum standards of professional conduct for attorneys who appear and practice before the SEC on behalf of public companies. These rules impose on attorneys a responsibility to report "up the ladder" material violations of federal and state securities laws, breaches of fiduciary duty, and other similar violations of federal and state laws. Second, the rules describe the internal steps to be followed by a company when an attorney reports an alleged material violation of federal and state securities laws. Third, they introduce a new board committee, the qualified legal compliance committee, as an alternative recipient of an attorney's report of evidence of a material violation. Last, they clarify when foreign attorneys must make such reports and when foreign attorneys are exempt from the new reporting obligations.

The rules apply to attorneys of reporting companies, both in-house counsel and outside counsel.[1] Additionally, the rules address the responsibilities of supervisory attorneys and subordinate attorneys for reporting material violations of securities laws.

Additionally, the SEC has proposed other rules that address an attorney's obligation to report securities law violations to the SEC (i.e., "reporting out" to third parties). The SEC has solicited comments to these proposed "noisy withdrawal" proposals, none of which are final or effective at the time of this writing.

THE ATTORNEY'S REPORTING OBLIGATION

When an attorney appearing or practicing before the SEC in the representation of a company becomes aware of credible evidence of a material violation of U.S. federal or state securities laws, a material breach of fiduciary duty under U.S. federal or state law, or a similar material violation of any other U.S. federal or state law by a company or any of its officers, directors, employees, or agents, that attorney has a reporting obligation. An attorney with a reporting obligation must immediately bring the evidence of a material violation to the company's chief legal officer, to both the company's chief legal officer and its chief executive officer, or to the company's qualified legal compliance committee, if such a committee has previously been established.[2]

TO WHOM DOES AN ATTORNEY OWE A RESPONSIBILITY?

An attorney owes his or her professional and ethical duties to the company as an organization, rather than to a company's officers, directors, or employees. This rule clarifies that an attorney advising the officers, directors, or employees of a company in the course of representing the company owes his or her duty to the organization as a whole, rather than to the officers, directors, or employees in question.

AN ATTORNEY'S REPORTING OBLIGATION

THE GENERAL REPORTING REGIME

STEP ONE: REPORT TO THE CLO OR CLO AND CEO. When an attorney appearing and practicing before the SEC (in the representation of a company) becomes aware of evidence of a material violation, that attorney must report the evidence to the company's chief legal officer, to both to the company's chief legal officer and its chief executive officer, or (as described below) to a qualified legal compliance committee.

If the reporting attorney reasonably believes that it would be futile to make such a report to a company's chief legal officer and chief executive officer, the attorney can bypass those officers and report to the audit committee or to another committee consisting solely of independent directors or, if there is no such committee, to the full board.

STEP TWO: INQUIRY AND RESPONSE BY THE CLO. After receiving such a report, a company's chief legal officer must make an inquiry that he or she reasonably believes is appropriate to determine if the alleged material violation has occurred, is ongoing, or is about to occur. Upon the conclusion of the inquiry, if the chief legal officer determines that no material violation has occurred, he or she may advise the reporting attorney of that determination and of the basis therefore. Otherwise, the chief legal officer must take all reasonable steps to cause the company to adopt an appropriate response and advise the reporting attorney accordingly.

STEP THREE: TAKING THE REPORT "UP THE LADDER." No further action is required of a reporting attorney if he or she receives an appropriate response within a reasonable period of time.

If the reporting attorney does not receive a response or does not believe that the chief legal officer or the chief executive officer of a company has provided an appropriate response within a reasonable time, the attorney must explain his or her reasons to the chief legal officer and chief executive officer (or their equivalents) and directors to whom the report was made and report the previously reported evidence of a material violation "up the ladder" as follows:

1. To the audit committee of the company's board of directors

2. If the company does not have an audit committee, to another committee of the board of directors composed solely of independent directors

3. If the company has neither of the foregoing committees, to the company's full board of directors

The rules also provide that if an attorney reasonably believes that he or she was discharged from employment or a retainer with a company as a result of making a report under the rules, he or she may so notify the company's board or any committee of the board.

THE QUALIFIED LEGAL COMPLIANCE COMMITTEE REGIME

FOR AN ATTORNEY. When an attorney appearing and practicing before the SEC in the representation of a company becomes aware of evidence of a material violation, instead of making a report in the manner previously described under Step Two, the attorney may report the evidence to the company's qualified legal compliance committee, if such a committee was established before the report in question. By making such a report, the attorney has entirely satisfied his or her reporting obligation and is not required to assess the response of the company or its qualified legal compliance committee to the report. Therefore, by establishing a qualified legal compliance committee, a company can avoid having to satisfy its attorneys as to the appropriateness and the adequacy of the company's response to reports of evidence of a material violation.

FOR A CHIEF LEGAL OFFICER. After receiving an attorney's report of evidence of a material violation, instead of making an inquiry in the manner previously described under Step Two, a company's chief legal officer may refer the report to a qualified legal compliance committee, if such a committee was established before the report in question. By making such a report, the company's chief legal officer has entirely satisfied his or her reporting obligation and is not required to assess the later response of the company or its qualified legal compliance committee to the report.

THE QUALIFIED LEGAL COMPLIANCE COMMITTEE. Under the new rules, a qualified legal compliance committee is a committee of the company (that may also be an audit or other committee) that:

1. is composed of at least one member of the company's audit committee (unless the company has no audit committee, in which case it must include at least one member from an equivalent committee of independent directors) and two or more independent directors

2. has adopted written procedures for the confidential receipt, retention, and consideration of any report of evidence of a material violation

3. has been established by the company's board with the authority and responsibility:
   a. to inform the chief legal officer and chief executive officer (or their equivalents) of any report of a material violation, unless the committee reasonably believers that it would be futile to make such a report
   b. to determine whether an investigation is necessary for such a report and, if it so determines, to notify the company's audit committee or the company's full board, to initiate an investigation to be conducted by the chief legal officer or outside attorneys and to retain any expert personnel deemed necessary
   c. following an investigation, to recommend, by majority vote, that the company implement an appropriate response and to inform the chief legal officer and chief executive officer (or their equivalents) and board of the results of the investigation and the remedial measures to be adopted

4. has the authority and responsibility to take, by majority vote, all other appropriate action, including notifying the SEC if a company fails in any material respect to implement an appropriate response recommended by its qualified legal compliance committee.

THE OBLIGATIONS OF INVESTIGATING AND DEFENDING ATTORNEYS

The rules provide that any attorney retained or directed by a company to investigate evidence of a material violation is generally subject to the reporting obligations prescribed in the rules. In addition, the rules specifically provide that the officer or director of a company, although an attorney may be retained to investigate reported evidence of a material violation, is not, having retained that attorney, relieved of his or her obligation to respond to the attorney who originally reported the evidence.

Nevertheless, an attorney is excused from the reporting obligation when he or she was retained or directed by the company's chief legal officer to investigate evidence of a material violation. The chief legal officer must then report the results of the investigation to the company's board of directors, its audit committee, a committee of independent directors, or a qualified legal compliance committee, unless both the investigating attorney and the chief legal officer reasonably believe that no material violation of securities laws has occurred, is ongoing, or is about to occur.

Additionally, an attorney will also be excused from the reporting obligation if (a) that attorney was retained or directed by the company's chief legal officer to assert in an investigation or proceeding a colorable defense on behalf of the company (or the applicable officer, director, or agent), consistent with that attorney's professional obligations, and (b) the chief legal officer provides reasonable and timely reports on the progress of the investigation or proceeding to the company's board, audit committee, committee of independent directors, or a qualified legal compliance committee.

Finally, an attorney will be excused from the reporting obligation if that attorney was retained or directed by a qualified legal compliance committee to investigate that evidence or assert in an investigation or proceeding a colorable defense on behalf of the company (or the applicable officer, director, or agent), consistent with that attorney's professional obligations.

RESPONSIBILITIES OF SUPERVISORY ATTORNEYS

An attorney supervising another attorney who is appearing and practicing before the SEC with respect to a matter, as well as any chief legal officer (or equivalent) directing such an attorney, must ensure that the subordinate attorney conforms to the new rules. If the subordinate attorney reports evidence of a material violation to his or her supervising attorney, that attorney is then responsible for making the required reports.

RESPONSIBILITIES OF SUBORDINATE ATTORNEYS

A subordinate attorney may satisfy his or her obligation by reporting evidence of a material violation of securities laws to his or her supervisory or directing attorney, provided that the supervisory or directing attorney is not the chief legal officer of the company suspected of the violation. Those attorneys who are supervised or directed by a company's chief legal officer must use one of the other reporting channels previously described above.

Finally, although a subordinate attorney may have discharged his or her reporting obligations with a report to a supervisory attorney, if the subordinate attorney reasonably believes that the supervisory attorney has failed to comply with the reporting obligations under the rules, that subordinate attorney may follow the steps and take the actions described above.

NOTES

1. The rules also apply to non-U.S. companies but not to foreign government issuers.
2. An attorney practicing outside the U.S. is required to comply with these rules except to the extent that such compliance is prohibited by foreign law.

EMPLOYEE WHISTLE-BLOWER PROTECTION

Section 806 of the Act creates a civil action for employees of public companies who have been subject to retaliation by their employers for disclosing illegal activities by their employers.

SECTION 806

Section 806 of the Sarbanes-Oxley Act prohibits a public company from discharging, demoting, suspending, threatening, harassing, or in any other manner discriminating against any officer, employee, contractor, subcontractor, or agent in the terms and conditions of his or her employment because of any lawful act done by such person to provide information, cause information to be provided, or otherwise assist in an investigation regarding any conduct that the employee reasonably believes constitutes a violation of any of the federal criminal provisions prohibiting mail, wire, bank, and securities fraud (Title 18 section 1341, 1343, 1344, or 1348), any rule or regulation of the SEC, or any provision of federal law relating to fraud against shareholders, when the information or assistance is provided to or the investigation is conducted by any of the following:

- a federal regulatory or law enforcement agency,

- any member of Congress or any committee of Congress, or

- a person with supervisory authority over the employee (or such other person working for the employer who has the authority to investigate, discover, or terminate misconduct).

It also prohibits the company from taking action against any of the persons listed above because of any lawful act done by such person to file, cause to be filed, testify, participate in, or otherwise assist in a proceeding filed or about to be filed (with any knowledge of the employer) relating to an alleged violation of Title 18 section 1341, 1343, 1344, or 1348, any rule or regulation of the SEC, or any provision of federal law relating to fraud against shareholders.

PROCEDURE

An aggrieved employee must file a complaint with the Secretary of Labor within 90 days of the date on which the retaliation occurred. If the Secretary of Labor has not issued a final decision within 180 days of the filing of the complaint, and such delay is not due to the bad faith of the aggrieved employee, the employee may bring an action in federal district court.

The statute provides that the proceedings before the Secretary of Labor are governed by the procedures and legal burdens of proof in the federal statute establishing the whistleblower protection program for employees in the airline industry.

REMEDIES

ADMINISTRATIVE AND CIVIL REMEDIES

If a whistleblower prevails under the administrative process or in court, he or she is entitled to all relief necessary to make such employee whole, including reinstatement with the same seniority status, payment of back pay with interest, and compensation for any special damages, including litigation costs, expert witness fees, and attorney fees.

CRIMINAL SANCTIONS

Section 1107 of the Act prohibits a person from knowingly, with the intent to retaliate, taking any action harmful to any other person, including interference with the lawful employment or livelihood of any person, for providing information to a law enforcement officer about the commission or possible commission of any federal offense. The penalties for retaliation against informants include fines and up to 10 years in prison.

MISCONDUCT, PENALTIES, AND STATUTES OF LIMITATIONS

CRIMINALIZATION OF MISCONDUCT

The Act makes criminal misconduct in the following two areas:

- CEO and CFO officer certification requirement
- Destruction of corporate audit records and/or alteration or falsification of records

CEO AND CFO OFFICER CERTIFICATION REQUIREMENT

Under Section 906 of the Act, all periodic reports containing financial statements filed with the SEC must be accompanied by a written statement by the CEO and CFO of the company, certifying that the report fully complies with the relevant rules of the Exchange Act and the information contained therein fairly presents, in all material respects, the financial condition and results of operations of the company. This certification requirement applies to all public companies for all periodic reports (i.e., Forms 10-Q, 10K and 20-F only, not Forms 8-K and 6-K).

Knowingly certifying a statement that does not comply with these requirements will be an offense punishable by a fine of up to $1 million and imprisonment for up to 10 years. Willfully giving the certification knowing that it is false will be an offense punishable by a fine of up to $5 million and imprisonment for up to 20 years.

DESTRUCTION OF CORPORATE AUDIT RECORDS AND/OR ALTERATION OR FALSIFICATION OF RECORDS

The knowing and willful destruction of any audit work papers or other documents related to an audit will be subject to a maximum penalty of 10 years in prison. Auditors of a public company must maintain all audit or review work papers for five years. Also the destruction, alteration, or falsification of records in federal investigations and bankruptcy proceedings with the intent to impede or influence such investigations or proceedings is subject to a maximum term of 20 years imprisonment.

INCREASED PENALTIES AND OTHER REMEDIES

ATTEMPTS AND CONSPIRACIES TO COMMIT CRIMINAL FRAUD OFFENSES

The Act amends the federal criminal fraud statute and provides that any person who attempts or conspires to commit any offense under the federal criminal fraud statute (mail, wire, bank, or securities fraud) will be subject to the same penalties as those prescribed for the underlying offense.

CRIMINAL PENALTIES FOR MAIL AND WIRE FRAUD AND FOR DEFRAUDING SHAREHOLDERS OF PUBLIC COMPANIES

The penalty for mail and wire fraud will be increased from five to 20 years in prison. The Act also increases the penalties under the federal mail fraud statute by subjecting anyone convicted of securities fraud or attempted securities fraud to a fine or imprisonment for up to 25 years or both.

CRIMINAL PENALTIES FOR ERISA VIOLATIONS

The Act amends the maximum fine for violations of ERISA by a natural person from $5,000 to $100,000 and increases the maximum jail term from one year to 10 years. Penalties for violations committed by companies will also increase from $100,000 to $500,000.

INCREASED CRIMINAL PENALTIES UNDER THE EXCHANGE ACT

The Act amends the Exchange Act to provide that a person who willfully violates any provision of the Exchange Act or any rule or regulation thereunder or who willfully and knowingly makes a statement in an application, report, or document required to be filed under the Exchange Act that is false or misleading with respect to any material fact will be subject to a fine of $5 million (increased from $1 million) or imprisonment for up to 20 years (increased from 10 years), if such person is a natural person. The fine is increased from $2.5 million to $25 million for a person other than a natural person.

RETALIATION AGAINST INFORMANTS

Knowingly and intentionally retaliating against informants providing truthful information relating to the commission or possible commission of a federal offense will be punishable by a fine and imprisonment for up to 20 years.

STATUTE OF LIMITATIONS FOR SECURITIES FRAUD LENGTHENED

The Act lengthens the statute of limitations for securities fraud. A private right of action that involves a claim of fraud, deceit, manipulation, or contrivance in violation of a regulatory requirement under the securities laws may now be brought not later than the earlier of two years after the discovery of the facts constituting the violation or five years after the violation.

BAR TO FUTURE SERVICE

Any person found to have violated the general antifraud provision of the Exchange Act can be barred by a court or the SEC, after notice and a hearing, from serving as a director or officer of a public company if his or her conduct demonstrates "unfitness" to serve as a director or officer of a public company.

THE ACT

Generally, a violation of the requirements of the Act would violate either the Act or the related SEC rules, which generally would be a violation of the Exchange Act, for which a broad variety of sanctions may be imposed.

Rule 10A-3 prohibits the national securities exchanges and Nasdaq from listing or continuing to list securities of a company that does not comply with the audit committee requirements of the rule, subject to providing an opportunity for the company to cure its non-compliance.

Under Rule 10A-3, each exchange and Nasdaq must require a listed company to notify it of any material noncompliance with the audit committee requirements promptly after an executive officer of a company becomes aware of the noncompliance. Subject to the opportunity to cure any noncompliance that must be provided to the listed company, delisting is required upon noncompliance with the audit committee requirements.

NYSE PROPOSALS

The company's chief executive officer must certify each year that he or she is not aware of any violations of the NYSE listing standards. The certification must be disclosed in each annual report to shareholders.

Upon finding a violation of a NYSE listing standard, the NYSE may issue a public reprimand letter to the company and ultimately suspend or delist the offending company.

Each company CEO will be required to promptly notify the NYSE after any executive officer of the company becomes aware of any material non-compliance with any applicable provisions of the Rule Proposals.

NASDAQ PROPOSALS

A material misrepresentation or omission by a company to Nasdaq may result in the company being delisted.

COMPLIANCE CHECKLIST

Rules	When Applicable	Applicability to Foreign Private and Canadian Issuers
Sec. 302 Civil Certifications by CEO and CFO.	Now.	**Yes.** Must include as an exhibit to Forms 20-F and 40-F, but not Form 6-K. Partially revised certification required for reports due on or after August 14, 2003. Fully revised certification (in-cluding certification re: designing internal controls) required for reports due on or after April 15, 2005.
Sec. 906 Criminal Certification by CEO and CFO.	Now.	**Yes.** Must include as an exhibit to Forms 20-F and 40-F, but not Form 6-K.
Accelerated filing (two business days) for Form 4 by corporate insiders. Mandated electronic filing and Web site posting for Forms 3, 4, and 5.	Now.	**No.**
Ban on personal loans or other extensions of credit to directors and executive officers.	Now.	**Yes.**
Material correcting adjustments identified by auditing firm must be reflected in financial reports.	Now.	**Yes.**
Forfeiture by CEO or CFO of bonus and equity compensation if financials restated as a result of misconduct.	Now.	**Yes.**
No retaliation against employees for whistleblowing.	Now.	**Yes.**

Rules	When Applicable	Applicability to Foreign Private and Canadian Issuers
Audit committee financial expert. Disclose in annual reports whether or not the audit committee includes at least one member who is a financial expert.	Now.	**Yes.** Disclosures in Forms 20-F and 40-F.
Code of ethics for CEOs and CFOs. Disclose in annual reports whether the company has adopted a code of ethics for the CEO and CFO.	Now.	**Yes.** Include disclosure in Forms 20-F and 40-F. *Non-U.S. issuers:* Disclose waivers during past year in Form 6-K or on Web site, encouraged but not required. *U.S. issuers:* Disclose within five business days of waiver.
Non-GAAP financial measures. Enhanced disclosure for press releases (Reg. G) and SEC filings.	Now.	**Yes,** but this additional disclosure does not apply to Canadian issuers using Form 40-F. Reg. G does not apply to a foreign private issuer if (1) its shares are listed outside the U.S., (2) the non-GAAP measure is not based on a measure calculated under U.S. GAAP, and (3) the non-GAAP measure is disclosed outside the U.S. (even if a contemporaneous or later public or Web site disclosure is made in, but not targeted to, investors in the U.S. or the information is later included in a Form 6-K).
Earnings releases to be furnished on Form 8-K within five business days.	Now.	**No.**
MD&A disclosure of off-balance sheet arrangements and aggregate debt obligations.	Off-balance sheet disclosure in SEC filings with financials for fiscal years ending on or after June 15, 2003. (continued)	**Yes.** Disclose in Forms 20-F and 40-F.

Rules	When Applicable	Applicability to Foreign Private and Canadian Issuers
	(continued) Aggregate contractual obligations table in SEC filings with financials for fiscal years ending on or after December 15, 2003.	
Ban on trading by directors and officers during pension fund blackout periods.	Now.	**Yes.** Blackout notices are filed on Form 8-K for U.S. issuers and as exhibits to Forms 20-F or 40-F for foreign private and Canadian issuers.
Strengthened auditor independence requirements and record retention. Additional circumstances where auditors lose independence, are prohibited from providing some non-audit services, pre-approval required for some services, rotation periods for audit partners, auditor report to audit committee of critical accounting policies, and alternative GAAP treatment and retention of audit papers.	Auditor independence requirements began May 6, 2003, subject to various transition periods. Record retention requirements began October 31, 2003.	**Yes.** Generally applies to foreign private issuers and foreign accounting firms that conduct audits of (1) foreign private issuers and (2) foreign subsidiaries or affiliates of U.S. issuers.
Attorney conduct rules. Attorneys appearing and practicing before the SEC must report material violations of securities law or fiduciary duties by a client issuer "up the ladder."	Now.	A "non-appearing foreign attorney" is (1) admitted to practice law outside the U.S., (2) does not hold himself or herself out as practicing U.S. federal or state securities law, and (3) conducts activities that could constitute appearing and practicing before the SEC only incidentally to, and in the ordinary course of, the foreign law practice or only in consultation with a U.S. attorney.

Rules	When Applicable	Applicability to Foreign Private and Canadian Issuers
Accelerated filing deadlines for Forms 10-Ks and 10-Qs: 60 (from 90) and 30 (from 45) days after period end.	Phased in over three years.	**No,** but the SEC is considering accelerating Form 20-F filing deadlines.
Web site posting of Exchange Act reports. Disclose whether posting and, if not, why not.	Now.	**No.**
Management assessment of internal controls. Would extend disclosure to management evaluation of internal controls. Would require annual evaluation and attestation by auditors of internal controls.	Effective for annual reports for fiscal years ending on or after April 15, 2005.	Disclosure is required annually in Forms 20-F and 40-F.
Audit Committee Disclosure, Independence, Responsibilities and Authority, and Procedures for Handling Complaints. For implementation by Exchanges and NASD.	SEC issued final rules on April 9, 2003; Exchanges and NASD must implement rules through listing standards to be approved by the SEC by December 1, 2003. Non-U.S. issuers must comply by July 31, 2005.	**Yes.** Applies to foreign private issuers, subject to exemptions from certain provisions to address special home country requirements. Disclosure in Forms 20-F and 40-F.
Improper influence of auditors. Prohibits any officer or director, or anyone acting under their direction, from improperly influencing auditors if such person knows or should know that his or her action could render the issuer's financial statements materially misleading.	Now.	**Yes.**
Disclosure of audit fees.	Annual reports for fiscal years ending on or after December 15, 2003.	**Yes.** Disclose in Forms 20-F and 40-F.

Rules	When Applicable	Applicability to Foreign Private and Canadian Issuers
Shareholder approval of equity compensation plans. Generally, the NYSE rule requires shareholder approval of all equity compensation plans and material plan revisions. Plans adopted before June 30, 2003 do not require shareholder approval unless they are materially revised. Additionally, brokers may not give a proxy to vote on equity compensation plans unless the beneficial owners have given voting instructions.	Now.	**No,** provided that the foreign private issuer provides the NYSE with a local counsel opinion that the company's governance practices comply with home country law and the rules of the principal non-U.S. securities market for the company's stock.

INDEX